W9-CBD-402

THE 6 PHASE
MEDITATION METHOD

ALSO BY VISHEN LAKHIANI

The Buddha and the Badass
The Code of the Extraordinary Mind

THE 6 PHASE MEDITATION METHOD

The Proven Technique to
Supercharge Your Mind, Manifest Your Goals,
and Make Magic in Minutes a Day

Vishen Lakhiani

RODALE
NEW YORK

Copyright © 2022 by Vishen Lakhiani

All rights reserved.

Published in the United States by Rodale Books, an imprint of Random House, a division of Penguin Random House LLC, New York.
RodaleBooks.com
RandomHouseBooks.com

RODALE and the Plant colophon are registered trademarks of Penguin Random House LLC.

Library of Congress Cataloging-in-Publication Data has been applied for.

"Happiness in the Now/Vision for the Future" graph on page 17 was originally published in *The Code of the Extraordinary Mind* by Vishen Lakhiani (New York: Rodale, 2016).

ISBN 978-0-593-23464-8
Ebook ISBN 978-0-593-23465-5
International ISBN 978-0-593-58023-3

Printed in the United States of America

Book design by Andrea Lau
Jacket design by Pete Garceau
Jacket photograph by Paulius Staniunas | All Is Amazing

10 9 8 7 6 5 4 3 2 1

First Edition

To Hayden and Eve. First and foremost.
And to my family, Kristina, Roope, Liubov, Mohan, Virgo.
For my team at Mindvalley and all the amazing authors and
students across the world who we live to serve.

CONTENTS

PREFACE

On September 19, 2019, several friends reached out with the following messages:

> Hey, congratulations, read about it in the press!
> You must be so proud.
> How cool!

I'd just woken up. *Wait, what?*

I had absolutely no idea what they were congratulating me for. It was a totally average day for me, as was the day before. I sat up in bed in my then-apartment in Kuala Lumpur, Malaysia, meditated, made myself a protein shake, showered, and took an Uber to work.

But the messages kept coming.

It turned out that my name had appeared in the press that morning—in reference to winning the US Open.

Now don't get ahead of yourself; I myself didn't win squat.

But a Romanian-Canadian teen by the name of Bianca Andreescu had. Beating Serena Williams in a nail-biting tennis major, she'd claimed her first Grand Slam title, and the world had been celebrating her ever since.

Furthermore, the bubbly nineteen-year-old had wiped the floor with Serena in the most gracious, positive, gentle way possible. She'd shaken her hand and even apologized for her victory!

The press got wind of this and found both her talent and her maturity fascinating, asking, quite simply, "How did you pull it off?"

Bianca allegedly smiled and responded, "Let me show you!"

That's where I come into the story. She pulled out her phone and flashed them my first book, *The Code of the Extraordinary Mind.*

I'd mentioned the 6 Phase Meditation protocol in my first bestseller, and since reading about it, Bianca had signed up for a seminar on the 6 Phase to start using it strategically to improve her performance and optimize her life. Every day she would visualize herself winning the US Open (a protocol you'll learn in Phase 4). And look where it got her.

So will you too win the US Open upon finishing this book? Probably not. These chapters won't cover how to win tennis matches. But what I can tell you is that you'll learn to win at life, crushing the goals that are most important to you as an individual.

Bianca is one of the millions of people who use the 6 Phase Meditation to feel and perform at their best and achieve the unimaginable.

She isn't the only high-profile athlete who uses the 6 Phase, either. So does Tony Gonzalez, the NFL Top 100 Hall of Famer, who credits this meditation in multiple press articles. As does Reggie Jackson of the LA Clippers, as well as his entire family (you can watch interviews with all of these amazing folks on my Instagram @vishen).

But the 6 Phase isn't just for athletes. It's used by artists, entrepreneurs, musicians, singers, and Hollywood stars whose movies you've probably seen.

Take *War & Leisure* singer-songwriter Miguel, for instance. *Billboard* magazine wrote a fascinating article about Miguel's meditation practice with his entire crew before major concerts, titled "Miguel Talks Connecting with Fans Through Meditation Before His Shows." Which meditation? *Billboard* asked.

Miguel responded, "It is a six-phase guided meditation narrated by Vishen Lakhiani that traverses consciousness, gratitude, forgiveness, three-year aspirations, visualization of one's perfect day, etc. . . . And the meditation lasts about 20 mins."

The reason rock stars and athletes apply the 6 Phase is that they instantly notice its effects. Whether the measure is audience applause or scoring more points, they all witness the same boost in performance.

Are you a world-famous athlete or artist? Maybe not. But do you have dreams and aspirations of what you want to bring to the world? Most probably, yes.

Even if you've never classed yourself as one before, you may well be an entrepreneur. You may well be a creative changemaker who's been waiting for a lucky break.

Your success might not be as obvious as Bianca's. As you go through your day, there won't be a scoreboard and a referee watching your every move. Nor will there be a live audience dancing and applauding your performance. But you'll feel it. It may be the gradual increase in sales that you notice first. Or perhaps you perceive that you're beginning to operate more frequently from a state of total flow. Perhaps, when you come to the end of your day, you're amazed at how much you got done with so little effort while still feeling fully energized. For many entrepreneurs and CEOs, the 6 Phase Meditation has become their most important daily practice.

Mark my words: By the end of this book you'll have all the tools you need to live the best, most successful, happiest life yet. And the people around you will notice.

This is why I'm so excited to deliver this protocol to you.

So what actually is the 6 Phase Meditation? Well, first off, it's not a traditional meditation. Let's dump that idea right here.

Rather, it's a series of science-backed mental scripts that you run in your head to transform the way you think about yourself and the world.

But before I dive deeper into the six phases, let me tell you about how I got obsessed with the power of the human mind and ended up starting one of the world's biggest companies in personal growth and human transformation—Mindvalley.

Bill Gates, Microsoft, and the Musty Sofa

You should know that I was never meant to be a meditation instructor. My life wasn't destined to be "spiritual," and I never for a second entertained the idea that one day I'd be writing bestselling books on the subject of human potential.

I was born in Malaysia and grew up in a huge Hindu family that held academia in the highest regard. If, like me, you have Indian immigrant heritage, you're familiar with the notion that you have four choices of career: you'll be an engineer, a doctor, a lawyer, or a family failure. No more, no less.

I'll always remember the way my grandfather looked at me as we were on a drive one Sunday afternoon. This was around the time Bill Gates had visited India, and it coincided with the month I was faced with the most important decision of my life so far: which subject to study in college.

Bill Gates's face was everywhere, on every news channel, in every paper. Inspired by the radio station blasting from the speakers, my grandfather had a light bulb moment, one that would dictate my choices for the five years ahead of me.

"Vishen," he said, looking me in the eyes with hope. "You must be rich like Bill Gates! You must know computers!"

As a teen with taped-up glasses who'd struggled with self-esteem issues most of his life, it's safe to say that I was more than eager to prove myself. I moved to the United States in the summer of 1999 and enrolled in the computer engineering program at the University of Michigan, Ann Arbor. It was one of the top five schools in the world for computer science at that time. After fully immersing myself in the American college culture (do I have to say more?) and graduating, I got my happily-ever-after. I landed the internship of my family's dreams: a role at Microsoft in Redmond, Washington.

That's right. I worked for Bill Gates. But as you have probably guessed by now, I didn't stick it out for all that long. I actually got myself fired on purpose. Here's what went down.

Despite the family praise and the temporary sense of achievement, two months in, I was miserable.

I'd wake up in the morning and hit the snooze button. Again and again and again. Although I'd become "successful," my soul was collapsing in on itself with the monotony. I remember one time when Bill Gates invited all the new hires to his gorgeous mansion overlooking Lake Washington. All my colleagues gathered around him and his BBQ grill as he served us freshly grilled burgers. There they were, beaming as they shook the hand of their hero. I was the only one at the gathering who couldn't do it. I knew I didn't belong. Bill was a gracious host and a brilliant man. But this world was not for me.

So I decided I was going to quit, but the sheer fear of disappointing my family was giving me cold sweats at night. I couldn't just walk out of there. I'd have to make it look like it wasn't my choice. So I hatched a plan to get myself fired.

I shut the doors of my office and played the game *Age of Empires* all day long until someone noticed. Low, I know. I got officially fired for "playing computer games during company hours."

I then moved to Silicon Valley with stars in my eyes to earn some money doing something I actually enjoyed. I'd be an entrepreneur! Of what, I wasn't sure, but I was filled with illogical optimism. I wholeheartedly believed I'd forge a successful career—I had to. And Silicon Valley was, to new computer science grads, what Hollywood was to aspiring actors. I was in the right place.

But my timing, in a word, sucked. A few months after I moved to Silicon Valley, the dot-com bubble burst. Fourteen thousand people in the area were laid off practically overnight in April 2001, the exact month I was trying to get my company off the ground. So good luck trying to shop around an idea in that environment. It was bad news for my ego. But it was even worse news for my bank balance.

Months of trying to launch this company had resulted in nothing. I slowly ran out of funds and soon could barely afford rent.

To reduce expenses, I moved a long way from the Valley and settled in the college town of Berkeley, California. I had less than $2,000 in my bank account and absolutely no job prospects.

Luckily, I found an accommodation option I could afford—a college student's two-seater couch. Yep, I couldn't even afford a room. But a college kid I met through some friends in a bar told me I could rent his couch for $200 a month.

"You had many . . . couch renters?" I asked nervously as I set my bags down and sat, cautiously, unsure as to whether it could take my weight. It was a very shady couch to say the least.

"Oh, yeah, dude. They just keep comin'. How do you think I'm paying my college bills?" He laughed.

I shared a polite smile. In the bag next to me was my life. All my belongings in the world. I was $30,000 in debt and I had burned through the initial seed money I had raised from the Bank of Dad and it wasn't going to get much easier. Even with my computer engineering degree and steadfast determination, I quickly realized I couldn't just become an entrepreneur overnight, and that floral sofa wasn't going to rent itself. I needed money, fast.

I had to give up my entrepreneurial dreams to get a job. But I couldn't get hired anywhere. With the dot-com crash, jobs were scarcer than ever.

Every day I'd wake up with a stiff neck and fire out more copies of my résumé more times than I care to remember, in the desperate hope that someone would eventually employ me. My life was a mess, and I was going nowhere fast.

Finally, after eight excruciating months of rejection and my pride on the floor, my luck turned around.

Through a connection, I was offered an opportunity to interview for a small startup selling case-management software to law firms. But the economy was still sore, and most companies were refusing to pay a base salary. I read through the offer email.

Oh, God.

It was a "dialing for dollars" job. Selling over the phone was my worst nightmare. I was a graduate of the prestigious University of Michigan College of Electrical Engineering and Computer Science, for crying out loud.

And I was going to be one of *those* people. But what choice did I have? If I left the offer any longer, some other wannabe success story would take my place on that stained two-seater and I'd have to return home to Malaysia with my tail between my legs.

So I took the job.

My great responsibility was dialing the numbers of hundreds of lawyers around the United States in an attempt to convince them to buy our software to manage their firms. Each morning, I'd be assigned an area—say, San Antonio, Texas. After I'd inhaled some crappy cereal I'd walk to the San Francisco Public Library. Back sore from another sleepless night on my precious, musty sofa, I'd sit myself down for the long haul with the Yellow Pages for San Antonio. I'd grab a notepad and pen and write down all the names of all the attorneys in that area from A to Z. Then I'd start calling. All of them in sequence.

There I was, a Malaysian kid with the name Vishen Lakhiani interrupting stone-faced attorneys in the middle of their busy days to sell them software. You can imagine how that went for me.

Phone-slamming, yelling, and f*ck-offs became my daily routine. But don't forget that lawyers are usually pretty good with linguistics too. Many wouldn't just settle for telling me to f*ck off. Oh, no. Many were powerfully poetic and imaginative about it. Their descriptions involved all kinds of exciting medieval torture techniques using inanimate objects such as broom handles and chair legs. Their monologues would haunt my dreams.

Stumbling onto the Most Important Lesson I Would Ever Learn

I was failing and I knew it. I'd somehow ended up in *another* job I hated, but this time for a fraction of the pay. The American Dream had chewed me up and spat me out *again*.

So I did what anyone would do in such a pitiful situation. I put my instant noodles to one side and turned to Google: the hottest, most magical new search engine at the time. We were all still mesmerized by its ability to answer anything we tossed at it.

Why does my life suck?

Important and, yes, somewhat pessimistic. Seek and you shall find. Google gave me a host of reasons why life sucked. I typed on.

Why do I hate my job?

Once more, Google informed me about all the reasons why people hate their jobs nowadays. It was very depressing.

Only 15% of the world's one billion full-time workers are engaged at work. It is significantly better in the U.S., at around 30% engaged, but this still means that roughly 70% of American workers aren't engaged.

Wow. Well, at least it wasn't just me. I kept scrolling.

A lot of the same stuff—life is hard, work makes it harder, and so on.

But then I saw something. Something that gave me the faint hope that there could be a solution.

Meditation Seminar for Work Performance, Los Angeles

Okay . . .

Click.

The promises were pretty big. They claimed that people who took this class sell better and smarter, get more positive about their jobs, and achieve dramatic career advancement. *Could meditation really help me accelerate my sales closing rate?* I wondered. By this point, I had absolutely nothing to lose, and the only thing that would notice my absence was the crappy sofa I tossed and turned on every night.

I decided to take a chance and go. After all, if I didn't like it, I could just slip out the back and return home.

After getting on a plane, spending the little money I had left on a motel, grabbing a cheap coffee, and showing up at that meditation class . . . what I saw in front of me was my worst nightmare.

I was alone.

I was the only student in the room.

The facilitator shrugged her shoulders and told me to take a seat.

Fearing the worst, imagining how she was going to light some incense, surround me with crystals, and demand that I chant a New Age mantra, I sat nervously.

But it wasn't as bad as I thought. Turns out, this meditation technique was relatively new, compared to practices that date back centuries. What's more, it was created by a meditation expert from Texas. His name was José Silva, and he aptly named the seminar "Silva Ultramind." His scientific-spiritual gift to the world became hugely popular in the 1970s and '80s, and now, I'd learn it all one-on-one.

Amanda (name changed) would be my guide. Amanda was in pharmaceutical sales, and let's just say you could smell her salary a mile off. Smartly dressed, cool and collected with her designer glasses resting on the bridge of her nose, she broke the meditation stereotype instantly. Maybe I wouldn't be slipping out the back after all.

She ran me through the entire Silva Ultramind System in a single workshop. In just one day, I had a good handle on how to access altered states of mind through meditation.

José Silva's legacy, I learned (he died in 1999), was teaching the world mental programming techniques that broke the mold of traditional passive meditation. It wasn't about clearing your mind and forgetting your problems. Rather, it was about turning your problems into *projects*. You would learn specific mental scripts to program your mind just like you'd program a computer. You could erase bad habits, accelerate healing, and even manifest dreams. Silva called this approach "active" meditation to distinguish it from more traditional "passive" approaches.

I left that seminar with the most peace I'd ever had in my life. I had no idea meditation could actually be that useful. Nor did I have any idea that there was about to be an exponential rise in interest in the scientific study of enhanced performance through meditation.

So I got myself back to San Francisco and started my own meditation practice. I meditated every single day from then on (pretty obsessively, granted), using all the techniques Amanda showed me. If this didn't work, I didn't know where I'd get next month's rent, so I really went for it.

I sat down every morning and visualized my sales doubling. I felt the excitement I'd feel in advance and I'd celebrate hitting my targets as if it were already a done deal. I breathed deep and connected to my newfound relationship with my gut feeling. I started listening quietly for inner guidance so I could use it at work.

One big change I made was deciding to no longer call lawyers in order of their Yellow Pages listing. Instead, I'd relax, go into my meditative state, tune into my intuition, and run my finger down those yellow pages; I'd stop when I got to a name that "felt" right. I would call on only those names. By the end of that first week, my closing rate doubled.

The meditation helped massively with my stress levels too, so I was on the ball from the get-go. I used my newfound levels of energy and empathy to connect, *properly*, with whoever picked up that phone, which did wonders for my customer rapport. Guess what happened?

Two weeks later, my sales had doubled again.

And it didn't stop there. I then brought in creative visualization using a technique called the mental screen (we'll cover this in chapter 4).

A month later, my sales doubled once more.

I went on to get promoted three times in the following four months. I made vice president of sales. But that wasn't enough for me. I asked the company founder if I could lead his nonexistent business development division.

I was so good at my job that the founder of the company ended up giving me *both* positions. Vishen Lakhiani, twenty-six years old, VP of sales and business development manager.

My boss was thinking the same thing you are.

"How the hell are you doing this, Vishen?" he asked me, brow furrowed, arms crossed.

Meditation and intuition, I explained. There was a long pause.

"That's bullshit . . . but can you keep doing it?"

The Inconvenient Side Effect of Meditation

I stayed at the company for eighteen more months, perfecting my meditation skills and landing an astronomical amount of sales. But within that time something had changed . . .

Me.

You see, something somewhat inconvenient happens when you start to meditate.

You start to become a better person.

Your life becomes more than just a question mark over how to get rich and impress your parents. When you meditate on a regular basis, your focus slowly shifts from your own ego to something more meaningful. The most common but unexpected side effect of meditation is that you end up caring about humanity way more than you ever thought you could.

So after a couple of years with that software company, I felt a bit short-changed . . . spiritually speaking.

I was "successful," but I became hyperaware, once again, that my job felt pretty void of true value. There had to be more to life than this. Who was I actually helping, for real? What would my legacy be? Call me a hippie, call me New Age, call me crazy . . . but I decided I was going to quit my generously paid work (again). But this time, I'd do something good for humanity.

If meditation had brought me this far, maybe I could rely on it to take me where I was meant to go.

So there I was at my computer a month later, contemplating my next big career change. I'd come to a block of the highest order: an existential crisis. Naturally, I did what any other person would do at a time like that.

I googled my question:

How do I change the world?

Pretty much straightaway I saw this quote:

If you want to change the world, change education.—Nelson Mandela

Wow. That was fast. Thanks, Nelson.

But what did *I* have to teach? Let's be honest, computer engineering workshops wouldn't put humanity into states of eternal bliss. What's more, it had to be something I was passionate about. It had to be something that was missing from the education system.

Then it hit me.

My mind flashed to the scene in Los Angeles, with me alone in that meditation seminar room. That class had literally transformed me in a *day*. Why did the subject never come up in my $29,000-a-year degree at the University of Michigan? Why was I the only person who showed up? Where were meditation, intuition, and personal growth studies in the education system?

And the rest is history.

To cut a long story short, I became a certified meditation instructor under the Silva Ultramind System and taught classes in London and New York for five years.

Several years later I founded my company, Mindvalley. And at Mindvalley, I'm proud to say we've managed to bring meditation to millions of people. Today, Mindvalley is one of the biggest full-spectrum life learning companies in the world. We cover all the bases for what humans need for a rich life—mind, body, spirit, entrepreneurship, performance, relationship skills—and meditation runs right through the heart of it all. We've been voted one of the happiest workplaces on the planet because we practice what we preach. And at the time of writing this book, Mindvalley has become one of the most valuable personal growth companies in the world, with more than twenty million fans across the world and revenues approaching $100 million.

Some call me lucky, and they'd be right. I just happened to meet the right people at the right time, and I've been able to base my career on something I feel could change the world for the better. But it was all by design, and I thank meditation for getting me there.

There are, of course, hundreds of types of meditation. But what you're about to learn in this book is how to practice a condensed, hyper-efficient, magic-making, joy-creating, productivity-inducing, goal-smashing mega meditation: the 6 Phase Method.

I put the sequence together based on everything I've learned about meditation over twenty years, and it's based on a vast amount of research and learning. I've been able to do this because I have a special advantage. Through Mindvalley I've interviewed and gotten to know more than a thousand leading minds in human performance, spirituality, and mind-set.

So what I've done is refine thousands of years' worth of psycho-spiritual wisdom, both the ancient and cutting-edge kinds, cherry-picked the best bits, translated it all into plain English, and put it in a logical order.

I ended up hacking meditation. Thousands of years of this-way-and-that-ing and overly complex scientific and spiritual research into *one* world-friendly, fifteen- to twenty-minute practice—the 6 Phase Meditation.

INTRODUCTION

I want to kick off this introduction with a statement that will probably confuse you.

I'm not a big fan of meditation.

Before you close this book and label me the hypocritical anti-Buddha, hear me out. Despite teaching *meditation* to millions of people, I feel that the word doesn't quite hit the spot.

So although I named this sequence the 6 Phase Meditation, and although you'll read the word a thousand times throughout this book, it's only because there isn't another comprehensive word that encompasses the process any better. Or at least in a way that everyone is going to understand and/or resonate with. And, let's be real, I'd like the people who are interested in finding some inner peace and living a better life to buy this book. From what I've seen, most people are googling *how to practice meditation* as opposed to *how to engage in variable multifaceted psychospiritual transcendent mind-training techniques.*

. . . so can you blame me?

"Meditation" is a snappier way to say it, but it's too general, not to mention stigmatized. It's like "exercise." *Exercise* is the umbrella word for cardio, weight training, aerobics, yoga, swimming, hiking, trampolining, and even pole-dancing, just like *meditation* is an umbrella word for a whole host of mental protocols. It's very nuanced.

Similarly, just as so many people dislike the word *exercise*, which conjures images of spandex, sweat, and thigh chafing, a hell of a lot of people are instantly put off by the word *meditation*. But exercise can be so much more than Zumba, and meditation is so much more than mantras and incense.

Furthermore, those who exercise don't have to be a size zero, and those who meditate don't have to be prayer-bead-wearing New Age hippies who stare into everyone's eyes for just *a few seconds too many*. (Although I myself have nothing against that; don't get me wrong.)

More on this exercise analogy. Sure, Zumba is good for you, but if you want to build muscle mass in your arms, it's probably not the best way to go about it. You'll want to lift weights for that. So if, for example, you're interested in meditation to quickly boost your levels of serotonin (the famous happiness chemical), you likely won't get there by clearing your mind. Check out a gratitude meditation instead. Want to feel loved-up and compassionate? There's nothing like a little loving-kindness meditation. Looking to hit sales targets? Try creative visualization. You get the idea. Radically different forms of meditation accomplish different things.

You really do have to be selective about your meditative style depending on where you're at and what you want. And that's exactly how I designed the six different phases; they're deliciously cherry-picked from all the best meditative practices to shape the greater sum of your day-to-day human experience.

Meditation: Then and Now

One of the biggest mistakes people make when they try meditation for the first time is that they throw themselves into the deep end of a very old, very specific meditative technique with no prior training.

Consequently, they end up feeling crappy about themselves. They search for "guided meditation" on YouTube to help calm their anxiety, and they pick one randomly. A few seconds in, they get weirded out by the eerily breathy voice telling them to "*just relax.*"

They get distracted by the cheesy image on the screen and the annoyingly repetitive panpipes. They try to clear their mind but end up thinking about what's for dinner. When the fifteen minutes are up, they're more stressed than when they began. Why? Because they think they're doing it wrong, and that their mind isn't cut out for being still. They conclude that meditation can't possibly be for them, so they never go back.

And why would they? If you went out on a Tinder date with someone who bored you to tears, looked nothing like they did in their pictures, and spent the entire time subtly shading you for how inept you were at dating, why the hell would you want to see them again?

That's what happens with meditation. You're told it'll make you feel better, but it's not what it's cracked up to be. So f*ck you, Tinder date. And f*ck you, meditation.

I know this because I've been there. Trust me when I say that clearing your mind and focusing on your breath while adopting the lotus posture are not necessary in order to reap the real benefits of meditation.

For us to truly understand where we went so wrong with the introduction of an ancient Asian practice to the West, it's probably worth exploring its origins.

Meditation is ancient. It originated in India thousands of years back. And they were really into it. They dug it so much at the time that the practice was adopted by neighboring countries pretty fast. It spread like wildfire and formed a part of many religions we know today throughout the world, including Hinduism and Buddhism. They used it as a way to obtain peace of mind and connect to a higher truth. They used it to disconnect from *saṃsāra*, aka the physical world, in order to connect with their true selves. They used it to get *enlightened*.

But the way people used to meditate in India some three thousand years ago is *very* different from how most of us need to meditate today.

Today you don't have the luxury of being able to escape your village at a moment's notice, find yourself a nice comfy cave, and stay there for six months if the going gets tough. Today you can't rely on your community to feed your kids while you're away chanting *om shanti*. Today you can't just stick a note on your hut door saying, "Meditating somewhere in the mountains, dunno when I'll be back!"

You can't just check out. Not if you want to maintain healthy relationships (not to mention a healthy bank balance). Life is different now.

That's not to say you can't reap the same benefits of meditation today that you would have a few thousand years ago. In fact, we need them now more than ever. Since 2012 the number of people practicing meditation has tripled, and that's both totally understandable and really positive.

But we're kind of getting it wrong.

We're missing the mark because we're trying to replicate those monastic practices within the chaos that is modern life, then beating ourselves up when we fail. It's like trying to fit a square peg into a round hole.

Remember that I opened this chapter by saying that I'm not a big fan of the word *meditation*? That's why. Because when the modern-day human hears the word, they think of monastic practices. And it can ruin the entire process from the get-go.

I prefer to use the phrase *transcendent practice*. In essence, a transcendent practice is any practice that takes you away from your physical outer world to make you go within. When I say "within," I mean to tune out the physical world and attune your attention inward to the mind and the soul. Which is important because we live in a world that's actively trying to stop you from doing just that.

Why? Because there's no profit in someone who has everything they need inside themselves, is there?

What Is the 6 Phase Meditation?

The 6 Phase Meditation is a transcendent fifteen- to twenty-minute practice that I custom-designed to produce peak states in its practitioners.

The 6 Phase Meditation puts six of the most powerful mental-health-inducing practices into one unified approach for the modern human.

I invite you to download the Mindvalley app to aid you on your journey. Access to the 6 Phase Meditation course is free with the purchase of this book. After you work your way through each chapter, you can dive straight into the meditation audio for the phase you just learned about. In every audio, I'll guide you carefully through the six phases. The book and the audio work together to lock in your meditation practice.

What I love the most about the 6 Phase Meditation is that everyone and anyone can use it *with ease*. It's simple and requires no special skills. But just like learning a martial art, where you practice a punch ten thousand times to get it perfect, the 6 Phase shows you how to fine-tune each practice to perfection as long as you keep it up and dedicate yourself to going deeper.

We'll dive into more details about each phase later on, but for now know that with each session you'll cover:

PHASE 1: The Circle of Love and Compassion

PHASE 2: Happiness and Gratitude

PHASE 3: Peace Through Forgiveness

PHASE 4: A Vision for Your Future

PHASE 5: Mastering Your Day

PHASE 6: The Blessing

While the 6 Phase is fundamentally a "meditation" (although you know I'm not into that word), it's heavily rooted in science and personal study. You get all the benefits of meditation without the confusion, stress, and outdated rules that unfortunately come with it.

It's basically a compilation of everything I've learned from interviewing more than a thousand leaders in the world of human potential and mind-set over two decades. It's the best, easiest practice out there, and most people who try it really love it.

I know this because I've tested it on millions of people. There's a reason athletes from every major US sports team, from the NBA to the NFL, are using it. There's a reason that rock stars, entrepreneurs, Hollywood actors, and the world's highest achievers are sitting down every morning and making the effort to slot it into their daily routines. Because, as you'll see when you try it, the 6 Phase isn't just about spiritual centeredness (which of course you'll get)—it's all about performance too.

It actively impacts the way you show up in the world, so you can help make it a better place.

So rock up in your pjs and join the club. No experience, prayer beads, vows of chastity, chanting, or incense necessary.

For Those Who Aren't New to Meditation

I want to take a moment to acknowledge the hard-core meditators out there. The ones who've studied traditional meditation for years, the ones who took out a loan to go find themselves in an ashram in India, the ones who are probably a bit pissed at me right now.

Please don't be.

Every single meditation you've done has been beneficial, and I don't want to take any value away from that. We're just approaching the whole concept in a slightly different, updated way. I want you to know that you too are in exactly the right place. Because it's my intention to bring the 6 Phase to *billions* of people, and for that we must make the lingo and the technique tangible for everyone. Nobody gets left behind.

Complexity should never be confused with effectiveness. And the 6 Phase is just that—it's effective. It's fully optimized. It's a powerful mental training practice. And you don't need a set of special meditative skills to reap the countless benefits. So no, you don't need to disappear off into the hills to attend a ten-day meditation retreat to find peace (although if that's your thing, please continue to enjoy the respite—I like a nice retreat now and then too). You don't need to force yourself into the lotus pose for a knee-wrenching hour-long session. You just need fifteen to twenty minutes and a comfortable spot.

When it comes to meditation, the "longer the better" rule is a myth. With the right mental training, you can reap the same—and I repeat, *the same*—benefits in a fraction of the time.

The Minimum Effective Dose Model of Meditation and Exercise

The 6 Phase Meditation is kind of like Tabata training. Ever heard of it?

Japanese scientists introduced Tabata to the world in the early 2010s, and exercise has never been the same since for fitness junkies. Here's the principle behind it: four minutes of intense exercise can induce the same benefits as an hour-long slower workout.

It's all about the minimum effective dose for maximum results.

Why spend an hour of your hectic day sweating miserably in a public class when four minutes at home will trim the same amount of belly fat? By the same token, why spend ten days (and all your expendable income) on a meditation retreat when you can access the 6 Phase Meditation for free and reap the same well-being?

Understanding the 6 Phase Through a 1980s Computer Game

Most of us have played computer games before, right? As a kid who grew up in the '80s, they were my *life*. One of the best was *Rings of Zilfin*.

I'd grab the floppy disk every day after school, and I'd transform into a tiny character called Reis who was jumping up and down with enthusiasm on the tiny screen of my clunky desktop. I had a very, very important job to do.

You see, long ago, the Zilfins (awesome wizard-ish people) built an enchanted realm of peace and abundance in the land of Batiniq. They created two rings of great power that, worn together, made the wearer invincible. Unfortunately, the evil Lord Dragos had found one of these rings, and with his impressive background in black magic, he'd tapped into crazy levels of power and started ransacking Batiniq. If he found the second ring, the universe was done for. Who was the one little guy who stood between Lord Dragos and world domination? Me.

My character, Reis, was a young boy presented with the task of embarking on a noble quest to find the Zilfins (and the infamous second ring). Then and only then would he draw on his magical abilities to kill Lord Dragos once and for all.

As the unassuming Reis, you had to travel through this funky '80s computer land to pick up different magical skills along the way. Let's face it, if you're going to face the evil Lord Dragos and save the day, you'll need some special powers. So you'd play, constantly upgrading different aspects of your character in preparation.

Reis had to level up his speed, his charisma, his weapons, his gold stash, and his spells to even stand a chance.

Now, as a twelve-year-old, this game was awesome . . . But I eventually got bored.

I was an impatient kid, and I just wanted to save Batiniq already, grab a chocolate milkshake to celebrate, and be done with it. So I hacked the game. My geeky younger self went about teaching himself computer programming in his spare time, figuring out which different variables in the code were hackable so as to give Reis unlimited special abilities.

I ended up exponentially upping my character's endurance. I tripled the amount of gold I had in my sack just for fun. I quadrupled my strength. I tweaked my bow and arrow accuracy to perfection. And it goes without saying that I went ahead and upgraded my sparkling charisma by 30 percent, just in case some lovely virtual ladies happened to stroll by.

I then triumphantly proceeded to breeze through the levels, kill Lord Dragos, finish the game, and enjoy my chocolate milkshake.

As I grew older, a thought crossed my mind.

Could the *Rings of Zilfin* be a clever reflection of personal growth?

What applied to Reis applies to all of us in the real world. Just as Reis needed speed, spells, gold, and cutting-edge weapons to optimize himself enough to win the quest, I figured that we needed to do the same in real life to stand a chance at thriving.

We, of course, need *different* skills to win in modern life (so you can go ahead and put down that axe).

How many?

You guessed it. Six.

We need all six elements of the 6 Phase Meditation to win the ultimate prize of a deeply fulfilling life. That way, when we come to the end of our own game as human beings, we can do so feeling that we've succeeded in our quest.

In 2012 I made a simple framework, named it the 6 Phase Meditation, and started using it every day to level myself up. When friends asked me to share it, I casually put it on YouTube.

And then it blew up.

An Introduction to the 6 Phase

As you can see, the 6 Phase Meditation is another example of my hacking escapades, but this time it's less about killing Lord Dragos and more about clearing the roadblocks between you and your best life.

With these six qualities, we become the most extraordinary versions of ourselves in the present moment. They also equip us with the tools we need for an awesome future. And without Lord Dragos, aka the pessimistic, stressed, closed-minded voice pulling us down, *there ain't no stopping us now.*

Just like Reis collected his superpowers, here are the ones you'll collect along the way during the 6 Phase Meditation:

Phase 1: The Circle of Love and Compassion

We accomplish this with a protocol for activating deep love and connection. This is a hugely powerful tool. It won't just level up your connection with yourself—it will enhance your relationships with others and the world itself. This protocol turns you into a kinder, nicer human being. All human beings need some love and compassion in their lives (no matter how much they may deny it), so this is why the compassion category takes pride of place as the first official phase.

Phase 2: Happiness and Gratitude

This will move your happiness bar up a level each time you practice. And the secret to happiness is gratitude. Gratitude is the ultimate remedy for the "lack mind-set," taking precedence above all other mental training. It boosts energy, reduces anxiety, improves sleep, and, according to some studies, is the human characteristic most associated with feelings of well-being.

While it's vital to have goals for the future, it's just as vital to stop and appreciate what you've accomplished thus far.

Phase 3: Peace Through Forgiveness

This will take a huge weight off your shoulders and allow you to move on with your life as a stronger, better, more resilient person. Being at peace with the world and the people around you is one of the most effective ways to maintain blissipline (the discipline of protecting your bliss) as well as rendering you *unf*ckwithable* (more on this idea in chapter 3).

Forgiveness is a superpower. What's more, research is now showing that forgiveness can lead to unexpected and profound health benefits, including reduced back pain, higher athletic performance, better heart health, and greater feelings of inner peace.

Phase 4: A Vision for Your Future

It's hugely energizing to have a vision pulling you forward—a picture of how you want your life to unfold. This phase will allow you to fine-tune your long-term goal-setting game plan and discover the vision for the life you truly want to live (and it will help you manifest it too).

In this phase, you learn how to apply visualization to craft an emotive, detailed vision of your future and to bring it into reality.

Phase 5: Mastering Your Day

This will give you a sense of mastery over the day to come and help you achieve whatever you need to achieve. It also translates your future dreams into actionable steps you can take immediately.

When you see your perfect day unfolding, you're priming your brain's reticular activating system (RAS) to notice the upcoming positives as opposed to what could go wrong. But there's also a powerful spiritual ideal in this practice that results in faster manifesting, luck, and synchronicity in your day-to-day life. More on this in chapter 5.

Phase 6: The Blessing

We attain this by connecting to a higher power. This will expand on your innermost feelings of being part of a benevolent universe, knowing you're not alone and that life itself supports your goals.

You can reap the benefits of this final phase whether you're spiritual or not. If you believe that there is a higher power, you can call upon it and receive a blessing—a beautiful ending to complete the meditation. If you don't believe in a higher power, you can imagine that you're calling on your inner strength. That's it, easy. It takes thirty seconds. It's the cherry on top of an amazing experience.

The Art of Bending Reality: How Your Present and Future Merge

The 6 Phase Meditation is not randomly structured, as I mentioned earlier.

Some of you may have already noticed, but if you look at the six sections above, you'll observe that the first three phases focus on your past and present, and the last three focus on your future.

The first three phases make up what I call your Pillar of Happiness. There's nothing like the practices of compassion, gratitude, and forgiveness to facilitate your joy in the now as well as liberate you from the chains of the past.

It's these practices that facilitate your inner peace and allow you to tune in to a deep sense of wholeness. They allow you to break free from negativity and all that ties you to your prejudices.

But then there's the second pillar. You absolutely need both pillars held up strong to live an optimal human experience.

Phases 4, 5, and 6 make up what I refer to as the Pillar of Vision. This pillar is made up of your deepest intuitive knowledge about where you want your life to go.

It's about who you want to become, how you want to feel, what you want to achieve, what experiences you want to revel in, and what you want to contribute. It's about what you want to leave behind when you've departed this world.

Together the six phases look like this:

1. Compassion ⎫
2. Gratitude   ⎬ Pillar of Happiness
3. Forgiveness ⎭
4. Vision for Your Future ⎫
5. The Perfect Day   ⎬ Pillar of Vision
6. The Blessing   ⎭

Here's a poem I love that shows how these two pillars work together in a life well lived.

On his eighty-sixth birthday, nearly a century ago now, John D.

Rockefeller Sr. wrote a poem that perfectly reflects what life feels like once you nail this notion of present-moment satisfaction and working toward your goals:

> *I was early taught to work as well as play;*
> *My life has been one long, happy holiday—*
> *Full of work, and full of play—*
> *I dropped the worry on the way—*
> *And God was good to me every day.*
>
> *—John D. Rockefeller Sr.*

Sounds great, right? When you strike the balance between your Pillar of Happiness and your Pillar of Vision, you stumble on the secret of life itself—the secret that made Rockefeller one of the richest men in human history. And I say "rich" in every sense of the word.

The problem is, very few people have two completely solid pillars, and they end up falling into traps that are pretty hard to get out of.

The Negative Spiral, the Current Reality Trap, and the Anxiety Corner

This heading looks like a weird twist on a C. S. Lewis novel, doesn't it? But this part is key if you want to understand the importance of strengthening both of your life pillars in equal measure.

Take a look at the following graph from *The Code of the Extraordinary Mind*.

Give yourself a moment to plot where you think you might be right now.

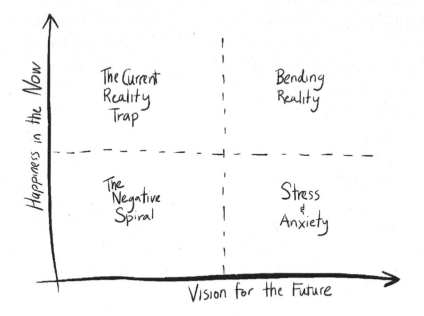

Low Happiness, Low Vision:
The Negative Spiral

If you feel like you're unsatisfied with your life as it is today, and don't have a vision for the future, you'll fall into the Negative Spiral. That's the most dangerous state of all, unfortunately. It provides the perfect breeding ground for depression and apathy.

High Happiness, Low Vision:
The Current Reality Trap

Some people have it slightly better. They're becoming at peace with their life as it stands. They start enjoying being in the moment and savoring the little things, which is great. They've solidified their Pillar of Happiness, but unfortunately, they've abandoned their Pillar of Vision. Therefore, they bump up against the Current Reality Trap.

This, to me, is a trap because your happiness becomes fleeting. It fluctuates with whatever is happening in the now. But true fulfillment is made up of both contentment *and* vision. It's through having a vision that your happiness can benefit humanity in an ever-expanding way. Not knowing what you want to do with your life or what mark you want to leave on the world renders you a passenger in your own life. You're at the mercy of the flow, and your state totally depends on the tide. You're a piece of driftwood.

Granted, you're a piece of generally *contented* driftwood, but a piece of driftwood all the same.

Low Happiness, High Vision: The Anxiety Corner

There's another group of people who lack a strong Pillar of Happiness, but what they *do* have is a vision. They might be unsatisfied right now, but they have a burning desire for change, for things to be different. It's great that they're motivated, but unfortunately, they often fall into the Anxiety Corner.

If you're constantly focusing on the future and pinning your happiness there, you'll be chronically unhappy in the present. It's called the paradox of intention. That's because your intention to be happy is making you . . . unhappy.

And the irony of that is the unhappier you are and the lower the vibe of your everyday life, the less likely you are to achieve your goals.

Entrepreneurs who are always after that next big sale, students striving for those high grades, and exasperated singles searching for love are some of the best examples.

If only they knew that happiness in the present moment was the missing ingredient to skyrocket them toward their goals.

In psychologist Shawn Achor's book *The Happiness Advantage*, he cites some incredible studies that prove how our levels of happiness dictate our performance.

According to Achor, happy people:

1. Are much more likely to achieve their dreams
2. Make for much better doctors, making diagnoses that are 19 percent more accurate than the norm
3. Make for incredible salespeople, landing 50 percent more sales than the average
4. Perform better than unhappy students on academic examinations

So there you have it—being happy in the present moment isn't going to have any detrimental effects on your dreams. On the contrary.

When you're both happy and appreciative of how life is right now (solidifying the Pillar of Happiness) and have a good plan for where you want your life to go in the future (constructing the Pillar of Vision), you graduate into the final category on the graph: Bending Reality.

High Happiness, High Vision: Bending Reality

I named this category Bending Reality because once you head into this arena, life molds itself in accordance with the person you've become.

Picture this. You wake up every morning in a state of gratitude for how your life is right now, and your visions for the future pull you gently out of bed.

You're aware of your mission, and every day you take steps toward achieving it while living fully in the present.

You contribute to the world, while simultaneously filling your own cup.

You're proud of how far you've come and rest soundly at night knowing that it's only up from here.

When you're in this state, life feels different. Almost magical. You're in flow—a state of heightened focus and awareness—and coincidences and synchronicity happen in abundance. The right people step into your life and the way you live life itself almost seems lucky. When you're at this level, you cannot help but believe in something greater than the physical world—because magic is a daily part of your life.

But to get to this point, you've got to make sure your Pillar of Vision is just as strong as your Pillar of Happiness. And that's where the 6 Phase Meditation comes in.

Remember, This Meditation Isn't About Meditation

For me, perfecting these practices as much as I can is my number one priority, not just in my meditative practices but in my life. It's thanks to the 6 Phase Meditation that I have deep, intimate relationships with my loved ones and a career I'm proud of. It's thanks to the 6 Phase Meditation that I can say, hand on heart, that most of the time, I'm a pretty contented person.

Because, as we've seen, meditation isn't actually about the fifteen minutes you sit on your cushion. It's about the real-life shifts for the better that you see in yourself when you get up.

None of us are perfect, and our flaws, as someone very close to me once observed, make us "flawsome." So meditation isn't about denying our shadow sides. What it *does* do is make you more aware of your inner jerk so you can notice it when it arises and attempts to wreak havoc on you and those around you.

Meditation, especially the 6 Phase, keeps you accountable to the highest version of yourself. It keeps you on the straight and narrow path to your unique vision of the future, your dreams, your values, and your aspirations. In short, this meditation sequence, if I do say so myself . . . is frickin' awesome beyond measure.

And I'm happy you're about to reclaim it and reap the incredible benefits without striving for unrealistic mind-clearing.

Let's address that last point.

Why You Don't Have to Clear Your Mind During the 6 Phase

Most meditation practices, in some way, focus on the goal of clearing, or at least quieting, the mind.

Now I don't know about you, but I've always found that a little weird.

Sure, it can feel really good to press the pause button on relentless thought patterns; I'm not denying that. But as Mindvalley meditation coach Emily Fletcher says, "Asking your mind to stop thinking is like asking your heart to stop beating."

Thinking, in and of itself, is given a pretty bad rap in a lot of spiritual practices, and the ego is often demonized. But there's nothing wrong with you if you find your mind goes feral when you sit on your meditation cushion.

After all, there's a reason ancient Buddhist scriptures depict the mind as "a drunken monkey jumping from branch to branch." The mind is meant to be that way—that's how it rolls. So while it pays to train your brain to calm down a little for your own well-being, there's more than one way to go about it. And just instructing your mind to "stop thinking" isn't going to cut it, is it?

That's why the 6 Phase Meditation is structured so compactly. As opposed to trying to block out thought, we're harnessing the power of thought to access the true benefits of meditation. We're not killing the monkey in a bid to find its bananas. We're training it to harvest them for us. Get it?

Emily Fletcher continues:

If we understand that the point of meditation is to get good at life—not to get good at meditation—and if we accept the reality that no one can give their mind a command to stop, then it's so much more innocent, so much more playful, and so much more enjoyable.

Now let's get started.

HOW TO PRACTICE
THE 6 PHASE MEDITATION

Ready to hack yourself in the name of an optimal earthly experience?

Then the 6 Phase Meditation awaits.

You can access it right now, for free, on the Mindvalley app, or the website (I'll outline exactly how to do that in this section). One of the best things about this meditation, as I said at the beginning of this book, is that it's suitable for absolutely everyone.

Nobody gets left behind or forgotten.

You don't need any special skills, you don't need any formal training, and you don't need those prayer beads, for crying out loud.

In fact, let's put the stereotypes to bed once and for all. I'm going to kick off this section with a list of things you absolutely do *not* need before becoming a "real" meditator.

Vishen's Official List of Stuff You Do *Not* Need to Buy to Become a Real Meditator

- Prayer beads, like I said
- Quartz singing bowl from Nepal
- Incense (don't be blaming your asthma on me . . .)
- Gluten-free everything
- Yogi teas (although, sure, I'm partial to them)
- Yoga mat
- Yoga socks
- Yoga block
- Yoga pants (Get the picture? Meditation is *not* yoga.)
- Crystals
- Tibetan throat chanting CD

I'm not done yet.

Vishen's Official List of Stuff You Do *Not* Need to Do to Become a Real Meditator

- Learn how to contort yourself into the lotus posture
- Clear your social circle of all "unenlightened" beings
- Go to India to "find yourself"
- Go vegan
- Start following a guru (don't get yourself into a cult on my behalf)
- Organize eye-gazing sessions with strangers
- Balance your chakras
- Become celibate

You. Do. Not. Need. To. Do. ANYTHING.

All you need is your fine self. Got somewhere comfy to sit? Great. Got a brain? Great. Got about twenty minutes? Great. You're ready.

When compared to a lot of dogmatized, monastic meditations out there, the 6 Phase Meditation is pretty humble. And I made it that way on purpose. It really is unfortunate that the people who need meditation the most (stressed nine-to-fivers living in the hectic modern world) are turned off by the culture that often goes along with meditation.

If you like the prayer beads, incense, chanting, herbal tea selections—please, you do you. There's absolutely nothing wrong with those practices at all. But what I want to hammer home here is that they're not a prerequisite for meditation. Especially this one.

Let's Start at the Very Beginning

. . . a very good place to start.

1: Forget Everything You Think You Know About Meditation

First things first—before you dive into your practice and get transported into heaven by my sweet, mellifluous voice—forget everything you think you know about meditation.

One of the most valuable, lesser-known keys to squeezing the maximum juice out of any new experience is to start with a very open beginner's mind-set.

So show up with a newbie attitude, even if you feel you've been there and done it when it comes to meditation. According to our

Mindvalley brain expert, Jim Kwik, one of the biggest reasons people fail to embrace new information optimally is that they're weighed down with prior "knowledge" about the subject. So when you press play on the 6 Phase Meditation recording, do so without expectations of yourself.

2: Decide When You'll Start Practicing

Timing is everything—especially when it comes to meditation.

So the second thing to consider is *when* you're going to start your practice.

If you ask me, the first thing in the morning is always best. There are a couple of reasons why.

First off, Phase 5 is all about planning your upcoming day, so if you're practicing at eight o'clock in the evening, you haven't got much of your "perfect day" left. What's more, meditating in the morning sets you, and everyone else around you, up for a nice twenty-four hours. Stock up on compassion, gratitude, forgiveness, creative visualization, and spiritual connection before you tuck into your morning omelet and you're onto a winner, right?

Second, your brain is in a perfect state (the alpha frequency) for optimal meditative practices *specifically* upon awakening. We know this because our brain waves can be actively observed and charted using a machine called an electroencephalograph (aka an EEG machine).

When you begin to meditate later—say, in the afternoon—your brain has to shift from the everyday waking state (beta) to this resting state (alpha). And this can be quite difficult for newbies to do. But if you start first thing in the morning, you're giving yourself a great leg up—because you're naturally in alpha anyhow.

3: Give Your Fellow Home Dwellers a Head's-Up

If you live alone, you can skip this bit. You have the unique setup for peace and tranquility at your fingertips, so being interrupted is not an issue.

But if, like me, you have kids, housemates, an affectionate spouse, or hyper pets, you don't have that luxury. So I think it's always a good idea to let whoever you live with know when and where you'll be practicing and politely ask them (or beg them) not to disturb you.

Do what you have to do. Promise your kids you'll play with them afterward or tell your spouse you'll make them breakfast. Just as long as they treat the fifteen to twenty minutes you're taking for yourself as sacred.

4: Decide Where You'll Practice

Then there's the conundrum of *where* to practice your meditation. For me, I like to sit up in bed as soon as I wake up and meditate there. I cross my legs and shove a pillow behind my lower back, but again, you don't have to. You can have your legs nice and straight with a cushion underneath your knees if you like.

As long as your spine is straight and comfortable and your head is free, you're in a good position to meditate. Bed, chair, floor, wherever. At home is the best setting, but if you're on the move, in a garden or park, or at the office, you can still make it work.

Just don't lie down, because that's a surefire way to snooze fifteen minutes into oblivion. That said, once all this becomes a habit for you, you'll be way less likely to ever fall asleep while doing the 6 Phase Meditation, even if you're a bit tired. Your brain will come to know the difference between meditation time and nap time. So for now, just sit up nice and straight wherever you are.

5: Grab Your Phone and Open the 6 Phase Meditation Audio

Now it's time to enjoy the 6 Phase Meditation in real time.

Have your cell phone close and open the meditation to begin. I recommend treating yourself to some good-quality headphones so you can enjoy the best sound quality. Even better, you'll get an extra special experience if you layer some binaural beats (two-tone auditory illusions that occur when you hear different frequency sounds in the left and right ears) or relaxing music behind the track. All sound options are available for free in the app.

If you haven't been using the actual meditation audio yet, here are a couple of ways to find it for free.

Option 1: The Mindvalley App

The Mindvalley app is by far the easiest and best way to access the 6 Phase Meditation.

Just download the Mindvalley app, create an account, and click on the Programs tab at the bottom left.

You'll find the entire 6 Phase Meditation program, including the lessons and the audios, for you to enjoy free of charge with this book. If you don't see it straightaway, search for it at the top by typing "6 Phase" in the search bar. When it appears, click on it to begin your journey.

If you've already completed the program and just want the 6 Phase Meditation audio, go to the Meditations tab on the bottom right. You can search directly for it there by typing in "6 Phase" again.

Once you find it, click the heart icon to make it one of your favorites. That way, as soon as you click on the meditation tab on the app the next day, the 6 Phase Meditation will appear automatically without your having to locate it in the folder.

Furthermore, you'll bag yourself an entire collection of other really effective guided meditations and courses (including amazing short courses for free such as The 3 Most Important Questions as well as more in-depth programs such as Silva Ultramind and Be Extraordinary—all will help you go even further down the rabbit hole of your potential after you're done learning about the 6 Phase). So go wild, there's loads there for free (and for the courses that aren't, you can unlock the entire collection with a Mindvalley membership).

Option 2: The Mindvalley Website

If you don't have a smartphone, all good. Go to the Mindvalley website (www.mindvalley.com/6phase) and sign up directly for the 6 Phase Meditation program to access all the material I just mentioned. The audio is available throughout the course.

If all this tech talk is confusing you, don't worry. It's super easy to use; you just create a Mindvalley account on your computer, on the internet. Then you create a login for free just like you would on your phone. The website is very much like the app, only . . . on your computer.

6: Take a Deep Breath and Follow My Lead

Now it's time to begin the meditation. I'll be guiding you through from start to finish, and you'll navigate the process just fine because you've gone above and beyond by reading this book first.

Remember, you don't have to already be in a space of calm and tranquility as soon as you start meditating. You'll get there by the end of the recording, so just meet yourself where you're at. Come as you are and enjoy.

It's going to be a very special experience.

7: Bonus Step—Mid-meditation Movement

Please don't suffer through any form of discomfort during this meditation in the name of doing it "properly."

Contrary to popular belief, you don't *have* to sit still when you meditate. Sure, it aids concentration, but movement isn't banned by any stretch of the imagination.

I know you've probably seen images from monasteries in India where holy men sit like statues all day, meditating in pure stillness. It really is a sight to see. Beautiful and unmoving, they render themselves oblivious to any weather, any sound, any insect that might land on their skin.

That to me, however, is a recipe for malaria.

Please feel free to move when you need to. If your leg cramps up, stretch it. If your child falls over, pick them up. Do what you need to do and then come straight back to it.

8: Bonus Step—When Your Thoughts Wander

The 6 Phase is a gift for minds that wander.

If you've been meditating for a while and have explored the "noting" style of meditation—the pure act of observing the mind and its stream of pondering—you'll know that most of our thoughts orient around two things: problem solving and planning. That's why the 6 Phase Meditation addresses these elements of thought directly.

That's a big reason Phase 3, forgiveness, is involved. If we're angry at someone and we try to meditate, the mind will always return to how much of a jerk they are.

That's survival mode, and it's totally normal. If we've got an upcoming event that we're nervous about, the mind will want to focus on it to prepare for the worst-case scenario. That's why Phase 4 and Phase 5 focus on forging a positive, optimistic plan for both the near and distant future.

See, the 6 Phase Meditation doesn't demonize thinking—it gives your thinking a fully optimized structure that draws on the power of the mind, ultimately improving your life for the long haul.

9: Bonus Step—Music

Another myth I'd love to debunk is of the musical kind.

You'll find a lot of hard-core meditators who claim icy silence is the only backdrop that should accompany meditation.

But I disagree. Again, it's like the lotus posture thing. If you'd prefer silence, if you prefer lotus, go ahead and do it that way. Every single meditator is different and has different preferences. There's no right or wrong.

But I personally dig meditating with binaural beats in the background.

Why?

Because binaural beats have been proven to provide some pretty surprising benefits. They aren't just some hokey tunes created by panpipe-playing yogis and singing whales. Binaural beats are created by a technology that plays two frequencies of sound—ideally, one in your left ear and one in your right, through some sexy headphones— that facilitate the practice of meditation by tuning your brain to their specific frequencies.

It sounds complex, but it's not, really. I'm going to tell you about a lab in Phase 3, the forgiveness chapter, where they study your brain waves. It's all measurable. Brain-wave frequencies reflect what state of mind you're in, and binaural beats help take you from the active, waking, beta state to a more rested state like alpha. Sure, you can totally get to that zenned-out, calm state of mind without binaural beats, but if they help, why not use them?

While playing the 6 Phase Meditation on the Mindvalley app,

you can actually customize the background audio to suit you with binaural beats and a wealth of other soothing melodies.

There you have it. Now you know exactly how to practice the 6 Phase Meditation.

Follow these steps, and you've set yourself up for a very productive session that will influence not only your upcoming day in a really positive way but your entire life. And I believe wholeheartedly that the meditation doesn't merely have the potential to change just *your* life, either. Rather, it's got the potential to impact everyone else's lives that are connected with yours as well. (I've got more to say on this in the closing word, so stay tuned.)

It makes me happier than I can say to tell you that you're about to join more than a million other human beings who practice the 6 Phase Meditation every day.

Welcome aboard.

CHAPTER 1

PHASE 1

The Circle of Love and Compassion

It is quite possible to lose one's sense of being a separate self and to experience a kind of boundless, open awareness—to feel, in other words, at one with the cosmos.

SAM HARRIS

Lift up your armpit and give it a whiff. Go on, seriously. I'm going somewhere with this.

What do you smell? Odds are, nothing too dramatic. In fact, you're probably detecting something borderline pleasant—the smell of minty fresh deodorant, floral cologne, or remnants of the shower gel you used this morning. Or perhaps all you pick up on is the sweet, succulent scent of your own awesomeness.

But if I'd asked you to sniff yourself in the same way in 1920, you'd have probably fainted. Because a hundred years ago, bathing wasn't exactly a priority. Your breath would have reeked too. Did you know that in the early 1920s, only 7 percent of Americans bothered to brush their teeth?

That said, we've made quite a bit of progress in the last hundred years, haven't we? Nowadays most of us are aware that hygiene is of the utmost importance. And when we shower and slap on some perfume, we're not just doing it for ourselves—we're also doing it in the name of other people's olfactory delight.

So why is it that while billions of people rock up at work smelling like a jasmine flower, most of them haven't given a second thought to their *mental* hygiene?

We wash our bodies daily. But we forget to wash our *minds*.

Many people, myself included, have woken up in the morning with feelings of anxiety, stress, or regrets from the day before. That's okay, it's human. But the problems arise when we choose to do nothing about those feelings. Because just like a bad smell, those states of being will also undoubtedly impact other people.

Whether you want to consciously or not, you're probably going to take out your frustrations on the world. When we're lost in an ocean of our own baggage, compassion goes out the window. We've set ourselves up for a bad day along with anyone else in the firing line.

Compassion: The Benefits

Compassion trains your brain to be kinder. And trust me, in today's world, kindness is a competitive advantage. But more on that later.

Compassion brings about an infectious bliss that touches everyone we come into contact with. As well as feeling amazing while you're practicing, compassion also helps prevent unnecessary bad juju from ruining *your* day, never mind anyone else's. Mountains suddenly don't have to be made out of molehills, because you get that, really, there's no difference between you and your fellow human beings. With the practice of compassion, you're able to see yourself in others, and therefore you can more easily let things slide.

Like when the waiter gets your order wrong. You know the feeling. That sinking in your stomach, that *oh for crying out loud* drama that goes off in your head when your steak isn't cooked the way you requested . . . sure, it's not the end of the world, but it's just plain annoying. You'll be damned if you give them a tip.

Now, I'm famously known as a great tipper. And that's not because I have an addiction to polishing my halo. It all came about as an unexpected side effect of engaging in compassion practices.

A few months back during a respite between Covid-19 lockdowns, a friend and I decided to hit a local café. And that was exciting because neither of us had had the luxury of eating out in a long time. There was a line of people just waiting to get in, and they were all happy to wait, smiling beneath their face coverings.

When we eventually were seated, I joyfully ordered a cup of coffee and a breakfast omelet with avocado from the waitress who approached our table.

Twenty minutes later, my coffee arrived. I took a sip. It was room temperature. And that, when you live in northern Europe, means *cold*. My friend, fuming at this point, sat back and tutted as I calmly asked for a hot coffee. Apologetic, the waitress scurried off to make me a new one. Only she didn't. She forgot.

Another thirty minutes later, my omelet was presented to me. But the guacamole side was missing. My friend turned to me, half laughing, half angry, and whispered, "The service here is awful!"

We carried on eating what we were given. When we were ready to leave, I smiled at the waitress and left her a twenty-euro tip.

"Are you nuts?" my friend asked, creasing her brow. "The service was ridiculous; why on earth would you give her twenty euros?!"

I'd not given it much thought. Granted, the service was pretty abysmal. But it was a hell of a lot better than being stuck at home on my own eating a microwaved meal. We'd not set foot outside for three months. This café was a godsend.

And that waitress? I didn't resent her. I genuinely felt for her.

That waitress was probably jobless for those three months that we were all locked down. All the restaurants and bars were shut down. As well as being painfully lonely like the rest of us, she probably had the added worry of where her next paycheck was going to come from. Maybe she had kids like me.

Then when she finally landed this job, she was told that she had to wear a mask over her nose and mouth for ten hours straight in an overcrowded, stuffy café. She could see the line of twenty people outside that she'd have to wait on straight after us. They were totally understaffed and all she could do was her very best to keep on top of the endless stream of requests . . . all the while living with the uncertainty as to whether she was going to lose her job, again, in the coming weeks.

So frankly, from that perspective, she was doing a helluva job. And maybe that tip, if nothing else, could buy her a well-deserved bottle of wine or a box of chocolates to unwind with that evening.

Because if it wasn't for people like her, working sporadically in hospitality during a global pandemic, we'd all go mad.

I explained all this to my friend. I got a polite nod of affirmation before we headed out into the rest of our day.

What I didn't tell her is that that very same morning, I'd completed the 6 Phase Meditation. And it looked like Phase 1 had paid off.

That three-minute-long meditation had made me a less judgmental and more understanding person. The Buddhists would say I'd been injected with a shot of "loving-kindness"—the antidote to the human tendency of "attribution error."

Fundamental Attribution Error: How We Misjudge Others and Make Excuses for Ourselves

You see, our brains are sneaky little self-glorifying devices that are precoded with this fundamental attribution error (an error that Phase 1 will free you from).

Let's say you're driving and somebody cuts you off on the highway. In your mind, you'll immediately blame them. You'll scream, "*What a jerk!*" (hopefully in your head, not out the window). In other words, you assume they have a character flaw: they're rude, arrogant, inconsiderate, and selfish.

But when you're the one who cuts someone off, in your head you'll go, "Oh God, sorry, sorry, sorry!" Whether it was an accident or not, you'll justify it. You're still getting used to your new car. You were tired because you couldn't sleep last night and you misjudged the space you had to overtake. You had to take your budgie to the vet. You had to get your daughter to school on time because it's show-and-tell day and you didn't want to let her down . . . fill in the blanks.

So when it's someone else, it's a character flaw. When it's you, it's just your unfortunate circumstances. You're the gentle underdog of the story who just made a mistake.

I got called an asshole once.

I was twenty-four years old and I was running through an airport because I had literally four minutes to catch my flight to the most important conference of my life. I'd been working at the time for a nonprofit organization called AIESEC that focused on cultivating world peace. I got paid a pretty shitty salary, but its mission meant something to me, so I stayed. I'd chosen the cheapest flight I could to get to the conference, and lo and behold, they'd changed the time of my connecting flight.

So there I was, running as fast as I could, gasping for breath and desperately trying to lug my huge bag behind me. If I missed that flight, I didn't know whether I could afford another, and I wasn't about to charge a nonprofit for it. In my rush, I tripped over a guy's suitcase. I got up and kept running, because every second counted.

As I soldiered on like a hero, I heard the words *"YOU ABSO-LUTE ASSHOLE!"* resonate through the airport corridor.

It was the guy whose baggage I'd tripped over.

And this perturbed me big-time. I'm genuinely not an asshole. I'm a nice guy. It was just an accident. But admittedly if someone had booted my bag without apologizing, I'd have probably thought the same thing about them.

There we have the fundamental attribution error again. I was an honest kid trying to catch a flight and save money because I worked for a nonprofit. But to the man who yelled at me, I was an inconsiderate ass who violated the peacefulness of his day. A young punk who kicked over his bag and kept running.

It was the same situation—but perceived from two opposite views.

Having a heightened sense of compassion dissolves that divide between "us" and "them." Consequently, you end up getting triggered a lot less because you understand that not everything is black and white. The perpetrator isn't always a villain, and not everyone is out to get you. It's not always a *character* flaw. Sometimes good people make mistakes, just like you do.

We all have bad days. Having a bad day doesn't make anyone a bad person.

But when those bad days with "bad behaviors" become chronic, that's probably worth looking into. And starting your day with compassionate practices is a great place to start.

The Selfish Side of Compassion

Now I've got to be honest. I didn't lovingly write the script of Phase 1: The Circle of Love and Compassion from a place of complete selflessness. It wasn't just out of the goodness of my innocent heart. Sure, it's nice to be nice to other people. Sure, those around you will thank you for it. But there's a more selfish side to compassion.

And if you can't bring yourself to practice out of sheer unconditional love for humanity, that's okay. Do it for you.

Because when you practice compassion, your emotional landscape gets a lot lighter, a lot happier, and a lot more balanced in the long term.

By inducing feelings of being more connected to everyone and everything, it goes without saying that you start seeing the world as a less threatening place. You start noticing how kind people can be. You begin to realize that the planet, with all its colorful inhabitants, is doing its best to work *for* you, not against you.

And science proves it. The University of Pennsylvania and the University of Illinois once did some incredible research on the effect of strong social connections on the human brain. Naming it "the Very Happy People Study," the scientists wanted to uncover the secret sauce behind profound *Homo sapiens* well-being.

Turns out, the sauce wasn't warm, sunny weather (although that helps). The sauce couldn't be found at the bottom of an empty Krispy Kreme donut tray. The sauce wasn't money, copious amounts of sex, or professional success.

The secret sauce was the strength of the participants' *social connections*.

The consistently very, very happy people who stood head and shoulders above the rest were the ones who enjoyed deep romantic relationships, family ties, and friendships. Simple. But you're not going to truly experience any of that without high levels of compassion.

The more compassionate you are, the deeper, more solid, and harmonious your relationships become. Compassion is the most valuable form of social currency there is. It's downright powerful.

What Is Compassion, Anyway?

Compassion, contrary to popular belief, isn't about feeling sorry for people.

It isn't synonymous with sympathy. It's all about loving *connection* with other beings, no matter who they are or where they're from.

When Buddhist monks meditate on compassion, they're not reflecting on all the woes of the world and chanting, "That's too baaaaad." They're connecting to humanity and, sometimes, with the Earth itself. They're feeling their place in it all and enjoying the oneness. They're practicing being in a relationship with *everyone* so they can rock up in the world full of unconditional love and peace. Now that's so much cooler than sympathy, isn't it?

Sympathy is "poor you." Compassion is "may you be well, fellow life form, because fundamentally, we're one and the same."

The difference is subtle but significant. Sympathy zaps your energy, and compassion boosts it. It's no wonder why Buddhist monks always have an expression of superior serenity on their faces—they went and discovered the holy grail of compassion way before we did.

That said, countless twenty-first-century scientists are finally paying attention to the topic and studying it pretty vigorously. They too want to know what compassion is and if it's really worth looking into.

Here's the best definition of compassion that scientists have come up with so far:

Compassion is the act of moving from judgment to caring, from isolation to connection, from difference to understanding.

That's an accurate description if you ask me. Something fascinating about compassion is that you can actually observe the caring, connection, and understanding in someone's brain scan. Lit up like a Christmas tree, a loving-kindness-trained brain even *looks* different from a "normal" brain, exhibiting more capacity for effortless positivity. Compassion quite literally rewires the mind for the better.

For me, compassion is simple. Compassion is the act of surrendering to a better version of yourself. It's about being warm and radiating that warmth outward. It's about genuinely caring about ourselves and other people.

As the great William Blake said, "We are put on earth a little space, that we might learn to bear the beams of love."

So what are we waiting for?

The Challenges of Compassion

Now that you know a little more about the benefits of compassion you can reap for yourself and others, you might be questioning why more people aren't talking about it.

Well, the way we're living life right now doesn't exactly set us up for success in the compassion department. Despite compassion being a natural side effect of being human (the vast majority of kids are born compassionate), society tends to train us out of it.

Let me prove it to you with an experiment.

Go look someone in the eye right now.

If you really want to challenge yourself, try to do this with someone you don't know all that well. If you're alone, go find a mirror and look into your own eyes. I want you to hold that gaze, as steady as possible, for one minute.

How does it feel?

How uncomfortable does basic, primal human connection feel for you? Rate it on a scale of 0 to 10.

If you live in the United States, Canada, Europe, or Australasia, you'll probably feel especially uncomfortable. Because in those areas of the world, people are trained to believe that human connection *should* feel uncomfortable. You were probably told that it's not polite to stare. Being stared at probably makes you feel extremely exposed and vulnerable. And that's so damn sad. It's not just a problem in those parts of the world, by the way. A surface-level connection culture has also spread to many other places in Asia, Africa, and South America.

But why is it like this? If the experience that most facilitates our fulfillment is socially defined as a rude, weird, and borderline painful activity . . . frankly, we're all doomed. Some re-learning *has* to happen here.

That's why compassion comes first in the 6 Phase Meditation sequence. Because connection shouldn't feel alien to us. It needs to be a strict priority in our lives.

Now I predict that 99 percent of you reading this book will have a question at this point. And your thought process may look something like this:

This compassion thing is all well and good, but what if someone is genuinely a jerk? What if I don't want to have compassion for the spawn of Hitler?

I get it. I hear you. We all have at least one person we wish we could materialize away from the planet for one reason or another. That's normal. And if this whole compassion idea isn't hitting the spot with a particular person, that's where Phase 3 comes in. It's all about forgiveness, which is kind of like industrial-strength compassion.

But for now, don't worry about it. I'll only ask you to concentrate on someone you love deeply and easily for Phase 1. I'll talk you through the process at the end of this chapter.

So even though Phase 1 doesn't focus on finding compassion for those who wrong us, it has actually helped me out in that sense too. Once I got into the swing of compassion, I wouldn't automatically blow up when someone pissed me off. I'd know what I needed to do to come to peace, quickly. My practice of compassion allowed me to take the reins of my mental health and work better with fallible human beings.

It did wonders for my personal and professional relationships, as well as allowed me to feel at home in the world, connected to everyone and everything in it.

The best thing is, you don't really have to try. Once you start practicing the 6 Phase Meditation on a regular basis, all this will happen on a subconscious level. It's like passive income. The good stuff just keeps coming.

Training Your Compassion "Muscles"

I know what you're thinking. Surely you can't become infinitely more compassionate and connected to the cosmos in a few measly minutes. Surely it's not something you can just decide to learn. Compassion isn't computer engineering, after all. There's no Duolingo to help you speak Betterpersonish.

Compassion is a personality trait. Either you are or you're not. You can't just make the decision to adopt an enlightened human quality, right?

Wrong!

Professor Richard J. Davidson and his colossal team of scientists, psychologists, and test subjects at the University of Wisconsin–Madison would agree with me.

Because these awesome humans proved that compassion *is*, in fact, a trainable skill. They too wanted to reveal the truth behind the nature-nurture debate surrounding compassion. Could it be learned and implemented? Or did your DNA dictate whether you were destined to be a reincarnation of Gandhi . . . or a bit of a jerk?

To answer that question, the team went about creating an extensive study on the qualities of compassion and kindness. They asked the participants to follow guided compassion meditations every day for two weeks. Done. No electric shocks, no pills, no pointy sticks or cages. The only responsibility the participants had was sitting back, relaxing, and cultivating feelings of compassion for different targets.

These targets included a loved one, themselves, a stranger, and someone they found difficult to be around. The scientists tracked their progress through regular brain scans.

Here's what they discovered:

These results suggest that compassion can be cultivated with training, where greater altruistic behavior may emerge from increased engagement in neural systems implicated in understanding the suffering of others, executive and emotional control, and reward processing.

To put that in plain English, what they found was that benevolent human qualities aren't predetermined. Rather, they are trainable. You can coach your brain into kindness. You can program more compassion into your kids. You can quite literally school yourself out of being a schmuck. Embracing a more compassionate version of yourself is a choice you can make. And practice makes perfect.

The Science Is In: Compassion Keeps You Younger and Sexier. Who Would Have Guessed?

So now that you're aware of the science behind compassion, and you know what's possible, let's dive deep into some random freebies that may surprise you.

Benefits of training your compassion muscles go way beyond surface-level serenity. Sure, you might get that "serene Buddha" look and feel far more connected to those around you. But the unexpected takeaways also include:

- Enhanced levels of optimism and positivity
- Development of natural generosity
- Heightened stress immunity
- Less reactivity to annoying stimuli
- Increased activation in the brain regions associated with bonding
- Reduced PTSD symptoms
- Reduced physical pain
- Reversal of aging

That's right. Compassion reverses aging.

Scientists at the University of North Carolina proved it. They led a randomized controlled trial to measure the length of the participants' telomeres (DNA markers of aging) before and after compassion practices. Normally, our telomeres are expected to shorten throughout our lives. Their length, and the rate at which their length reduces, gives scientists a highly accurate indication of how old someone is as well as how fast they are aging.

So in this study, scientists compared the length of those telomeres in people who practiced loving-kindness compassion meditations versus those who didn't. Incredibly, while telomere length was reduced for the nonmeditators, it did not shorten at all in the loving-kindness meditation group.

In other words, kindness and compassion slow aging at a *genetic* level. Crazy, isn't it?

Here's another very useful benefit of a compassion practice. If you're a single man, listen up—because compassion might just help you land your next successful date.

Studies show that the single most attractive attribute in a man from the female perspective is *kindness*. And compassion is the root of kindness!

Ladies, you're not left out here. A similar study showed that men also consistently rated women as more desirable if they embodied compassion to some degree. So despite their binary design, the studies demonstrate that the attractiveness of compassion is gender-neutral.

We're all biologically wired to be drawn to people who are compassionate. Have you seen the hordes of people who assemble in front of the Dalai Lama just hoping to catch a mere glimpse of his loving gaze? We all want to be loved and understood, and compassion is the secret ingredient that makes the magic happen. Why wouldn't we want to hang out with compassionate people?

Heart Resonance: The Health Indicator We Don't Pay Enough Attention To

I wanted to make Phase 1 more personal. I wanted to be able to actually *see* and *feel* my connection with the world, not just go through the mental motions. In my search for the perfect technique, I stumbled across the compassion protocols from the HeartMath Institute.

Based in California, the HeartMath Institute is home to passionate scientists who are fascinated by a concept called "heart resonance."

Your heart resonance is the timing between the beats of your heart, which correlates to your levels of loving connection. And you can measure it, develop it, and use it as a launchpad to feelings of overwhelming bliss.

Those scientists came up with a simple practice you can do that actually trains your compassion levels, or your heart resonance, to use their term. You can do it right now. The practice looks like this:

Think about someone you love.

Imagine them standing in front of you, smiling. As you see their face, tell them you love them.

Feel the depth of your adoration in your heart and stay in this feeling for thirty seconds.

Now, let me tell you what you just did.

The mere act of using your compassion muscles caused biochemical changes to immediately take place in your body. You've just done a gym session for your heart resonance that produced oxytocin along with other well-being-inducing chemicals. If you had a scientist with you right now, she'd be able to show you on a heart monitor as well as a brain scan what awesome effects just happened.

When I got wind of how easy this process is, I had an idea. I decided that for Phase 1, we'd start with the HeartMath heart resonance hack, then expand that love outward to encompass the whole planet. It proved much easier than trying to create compassion for the whole human race out of thin air.

So whether it's your spouse, kid, guru, or cat whose purr soothes your soul . . . the first step is to identify someone or something you love. No judgment on who or what you choose. As long as you love them, they'll work perfectly for this exercise.

Then we will use your loved one as a trampoline.

Granted, that sounds weirder than I intended. What I mean is, we'll use the good vibes their little face brings you to bounce off as a springboard. We'll recycle the love you have for them into the rest of the world. First to your household, then your city, then your country, then your continent, and finally, to the entirety of planet Earth.

Next, I'll outline exactly what you'll be asked to do during the 6 Phase Meditation. Don't worry about remembering this process by heart, because you can listen to me guiding you by using the 6 Phase Meditation in the Mindvalley app.

This is just to deepen your understanding and, ultimately, your experience on the meditation cushion.

The Circle of Love and Compassion Protocol

Step 1—Bring a Loved One to Mind

Take a deep breath, and on your exhale see a loved one in front of you in the most vivid detail possible.

See them smiling with stars in their eyes. If you're not very visual, just sense their presence. First, simply internalize the feeling of compassion by tuning into the love they inspire within you. Bring your awareness to your heart space, and give those feelings of love a color. It could be pink, light blue, green, whatever comes to mind. Allow yourself to marinate in oxytocin as you breathe deeply. Let them know how much you adore them, and cash in your one-way ticket to bliss from the get-go.

Step 2—Let the Compassion Encompass Your Body

Let yourself go from feeling compassion for your loved one in your heart to feeling the sensation all through your body.

Take a deep breath, and as you exhale, allow this feeling of love to travel from your heart space into every single cell of your body. Allow that soothing, colorful light to expand from your heart to encompass your entire system. Feel it form a comforting bubble around you. You deserve some of your own love too. Try your best to find compassion for yourself. As my good friend and one of our most loved Mindvalley teachers, Lisa Nichols, says, "Fill your cup first . . . only then can you serve from your overflow."

Step 3—Expand Your Compassion into the Room You're In

Now it's time to expand that compassion and connection into the room where you're meditating.

Take another deep breath, and as you exhale, see that bubble of compassion expanding. Imagine it expanding and covering every living creature in that room, including people, plants, and pets—no boundaries needed. For me, it feels really good to do this while I'm sitting up in bed next to a sleeping partner or family member. There's something really wholesome about it.

Step 4—Send Your Compassion into the Streets

Now that you've got the hang of expanding compassion through space, you're ready to go a bit further afield into your neighborhood.

Imagine your bubble of compassion spreading throughout your entire home first, touching anyone who lives there. Next, imagine it expanding to engulf your entire neighborhood. I like to bring to mind a random neighbor who suddenly smiles out of nowhere because they can feel the positive vibes I'm sending. Keep breathing deeply and maintain that feeling of love as strongly as you can.

Step 5—Allow Compassion to Encompass Your City and Country

Start with your city, then expand to your entire country.

For this part, I like to see a map of my city in my mind's eye that zooms out into a map of my country. You can see your city as if you're flying over it in a helicopter or viewing a drone shot of it. Visualize your city covered in the light of your compassion.

Next, expand this compassion until it encompasses the entire country. See it covered in the light of your compassion. Use your imagination here. Feeling that love in your system, take a deep breath, and on the exhale, in your mind's eye, share the love with the nation.

Step 6—Allow Your Compassion to Envelop the Earth

Here's where it gets interesting. Take a deep breath. From your country, you're going to keep sending this compassion out into your continent on the exhale.

Then make your way through every single continent for each new exhale: North America, South America, Africa, Europe, Asia, Oceania . . . even to the penguins in Antarctica. See your compassion as a friendly tsunami, washing over the entire planet. This is the final stage of the compassion practice that connects us not just to those closest to us, but to all life on Earth. Go wild. See people of all nations and cultures. See birds in flight, see the big cats, see rain forests and snowstorms, see sunsets, and way into the depths of the ocean.

See it all and feel your place in this beautiful world.

The last image you see should be the planet Earth, beautifully covered in the light of your compassion.

If you get lost at any point and lose the oxytocin-laden vibes you created in step 1, return to your loved one. See your nearest and dearest in front of you once more, charge yourself up with love, and spread it outward again.

It might take a bit of practice, so don't beat yourself up if you're struggling to share the love at first. Cut yourself some slack—you're part of the less than one percent of people who are training themselves out of survival mode. You're in the Compassionate Being Bootcamp.

Once you've got the hang of it, it'll become second nature. And you'll be one of those remarkable individuals who not only feel a connection with their social circle, but with all of humanity.

Imagine what that will do for your mental health. Imagine what that will do for every single person you come into contact with. Because, trust me, they'll feel your energy.

Can you imagine if all of us dedicated some of our time to compassion training? I swear, it could save the world. Think about it. Think about the most (man-made) traumatic events in history, the ones that nearly wiped us *all* off the face of the damn Earth. They all came about, to some degree, due to a lack of compassion.

Think about how many wars we'd avoid. Think about how we'd treat the planet. Think about how we'd treat our loved ones, the stranger on the street, and ourselves.

Now you know that compassion is so much more than sympathy. Rather, it's about creating a kinder world and finding your unique place within it. It's such a powerful attribute of humankind that it may well be our biggest evolutionary achievement. It's our silent superpower.

I resonated with Marvel's much-loved Viking superhero a lot when he said:

I would rather be a good man than a great king.

Same here, Thor.

When I'm on my deathbed, I doubt I'll be too concerned with how much power I've had over others or how much "success" I've had. Odds are, I'll be reflecting on how well I mastered compassion. Yes, I'll be thinking about how well I learned to love.

What about you?

Before you proceed to the next chapter, you might want to open your Mindvalley app and launch the 6 Phase Meditation program. From there, you can jump into the full interactive lesson for Phase 1: The Circle of Love and Compassion. The lesson is just a few minutes long and will recap some of the most important points in this chapter. Upon completion, you can then dive straight into the meditation audio where I'll guide you through the compassion protocol. It will take less than five minutes, but it will help lock in this first phase of your practice.

The lesson is optional. But the meditation is a must. Transformation happens best when we rapidly apply what we learn. Put this book down now and try the meditation.

When you're done you can proceed to the next chapter.

CHAPTER 2

PHASE 2

Happiness and Gratitude

I was complaining that I had no shoes
till I met a man who had no feet.

CONFUCIUS

What's humanity *really* searching for?

Scientific progress? The meaning of life? Infinite wealth? The elixir of immortality?

Yes. Yes to all of the above. But there's something even more valuable we can't resist searching for over everything else. According to Albert Einstein in 1931, in one of his many interviews, "It's happiness we're after."

Best known for developing the theory of relativity, Einstein was just as curious as we are about the elusive nature of joy. And just as he provided the world with revolutionary formulas in the field of theoretical physics, he also found an equation for happiness. And it sold for $1.56 million.

Einstein's $1.5 Million Happiness Formula

After traveling to Japan in 1922 for a series of scientific lectures, Einstein claimed to have been deeply contemplating the question of happiness during his entire trip.

With a backdrop of cherry trees and geishas, he found himself in the perfect place to connect with the true meaning of well-being. After finding the secret formula, he lovingly handwrote it in his first language, German, on a piece of paper.

Convinced of its great value, he handed the thirteen-word formula to the hotel's bellboy as a tip for making a delivery to his room. It read:

Stilles bescheidenes Leben gibt mehr Glueck als erfolgreiches Streben, verbunden mit bestaendiger Unruhe.

In case your German is a little rusty, here's the translation in English:

A calm and humble life brings more happiness than the pursuit of success combined with constant restlessness.

Einstein's beautiful gesture was worth its weight in gold. Literally. Ninety-five years later, one of the bellboy's family members sold that piece of paper for $1.56 million at an auction.

But what does it actually mean?

You may have your own ideas, but from my perspective, Einstein wasn't just telling us to drop our goals and settle for less. I'm a big advocate for setting intentions and having a vision for our lives, which we'll cover later on. No, I reckon he was warning us against the "lack mind-set," the "not-enough" principle, the striving, and the blood, sweat, and tears that block true fulfillment.

I believe he wanted to set us free from the widespread "I'll-be-happy-when" syndrome: the never-ending chase that brings "constant restlessness."

And what's the one bulletproof medicine to support us in healing from it?

The power of gratitude.

More on the "I'll-Be-Happy-When" Syndrome

Before we dive deeper into the science of gratitude and how it directly influences our happiness, I want to tell you more about the almost unspoken syndrome I just mentioned.

I'm sorry to be the bearer of bad news. But if you're a human living in the twenty-first century, you've probably got it.

And it's bringing humanity to its knees.

The ultimate peace-thief, the "I'll-be-happy-when" syndrome is the notion that attaining certain worldly pleasures or accomplishments leads to inevitable happiness. Except they're always *just* out of reach. In today's "thank you—next!" world, we're told that happiness waits for us on the other side of [insert pleasure/achievement]. But when we get there, of course, happiness eludes us.

We've all been there.

I'll be happy when I graduate from college.
I'll be happy when I find my new boyfriend.
I'll be happy when I marry the girl of my dreams.
I'll be happy when I buy a beach hut in Hawaii.
I'll be happy when I get promoted.
I'll be happy when I move into the house with the white picket
    fence.
I'll be happy when I have three kids.
I'll be happy when I eat this family pack of Flamin' Hot Cheetos.

We may feel short bursts of happiness when, after striving, we finally obtain these things. That said, the novelty soon wears off, and lo and behold, we're back to square one.

Introducing the Happiness Gap

The world-renowned entrepreneurial coach Dan Sullivan talks about this fascinating idea that he named the "forward gap," which refers to the classic human condition of dissatisfaction. We all experience this gap as soon as our awareness homes in on the difference between where we are right now and where we *want* to be.

The forward gap is the distance between our present satisfaction and the happiness we believe we will gain when we hit a future outcome.

We fixate on this gap, grasping at any chance to make it a bit nar-

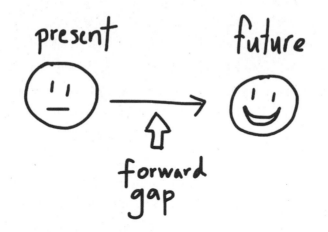

rower, bewitched into believing we'll be happy when we do so. But here's the thing. You were tricked. Because you'll never, ever be able to close it.

It's like running toward the horizon under the deluded impression you'll be able to touch the sun. No matter how fast you run or how many laborious miles you cover, the sad truth is that the heat of the horizon will never touch your skin. This is the "restlessness" Einstein was referring to on that famous scrap of paper.

Be honest with yourself. Do you ever feel like you're postponing your happiness indefinitely? That's the "I'll-be-happy-when" syndrome at its finest. Because even if you do manage to hit your goals, before you know it the gap will be back. It's a bottomless cup of desire we'll never fill. But we're addicted to trying.

If you feel slightly attacked right now, it's probably a good sign. I'm prepared to be the recipient of your bad juju in the name of your personal growth. But just know that you're not alone. I chased after that horizon like a madman for most of my life in a desperate attempt to close that gap. I had the "I'll-be-happy-when" syndrome, and hell, it still catches me out from time to time. And no wonder.

We were raised by parents who had already been infected, because their parents were, because their parents were, because their parents were. The idea that happiness is attainable through external means is far from new.

Yet there's nothing wrong with this, either. Progress happens because of our yearning, generation after generation, to make life better. This yearning has a positive aspect—it makes us *build, invent, create, improve*—over and over again as a human species.

But the great secret is to understand that happiness is actually the rocket fuel for productivity. And that we should be happy *before* we reach our goals. Dan Sullivan defines this as the "reverse gap."

The reverse gap is what you get from looking backward.

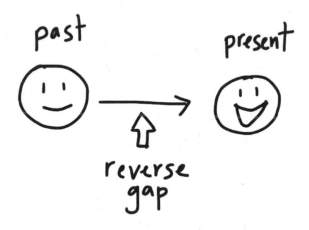

It's the joy we get from recognizing just how far we've come.

And you must embrace the reverse gap as much as the forward

gap. This is especially true if you're the type of person who is goal-driven or absorbed in growing your career or business.

Dan Sullivan noticed a "forward gap pattern" in hundreds of entrepreneurs. They were wonderful people with wonderful lives—yet they were harboring feelings of unfulfillment.

They had the "I'll-be-happy-when" syndrome.

They all believed their fulfillment was just around the corner. And they'd all fallen into chasing that ever-further horizon. They were trying, and failing, to close the infamous happiness gap.

So Dan suggested a simple flip of that mental model. His clients went to work on training themselves, daily, to pay attention not just to where they were going but to where they'd *been*. They reflected on the achievements they already had in the bag. They reflected on their triumphs, their happy memories, and the deep relationships they'd forged with their loved ones. They focused on what they had, not what they were lacking. But most of all, they reflected on how far they'd come as people and how they'd changed for the better.

They developed a calmer life, with less restlessness.

In other words, they began a gratitude practice Einstein would have been proud of.

How Did We Get So Obsessed with Postponing Happiness?

We live in a society that constantly reminds us how much happier we'd be if we bought whatever they're selling. Our happiness has a price tag, and nobody forks out more than someone with the "I'll-be-happy-when" syndrome.

When we're stuck in the forward gap, our consumerist society cracks open the champagne to celebrate. Yes, we're encouraged to be a bit unhappy.

Why?

Because there's not a whole lot of money to be made in happy people, is there?

Think about how many beauty companies would go bust if women woke up tomorrow feeling at peace with their bodies.

Think about how the electric appliances mega monster (that rhymes with *Grapple*) would crumble if people stopped caring about upgrades and started spending real FaceTime with the ones they loved?

Think about how quickly the pharmaceutical industry would go under if we started taking the reins of our mental health holistically. More on that later.

You get the picture, anyway. We live in a world that constantly offers ever newer, ever shinier solutions for attaining happiness through external means.

You grew up in this world. But you don't have to continue living in it if you choose not to.

The Rebellious Nature of Gratitude

Gratitude is by far the fastest, most efficient way to produce happy chemicals in your body from thought alone. It's about wanting what you already have, and celebrating it emotionally. It's about being thankful for the blessings in your life, be they huge or minuscule.

It's about being present where you are right now and raising a glass to all the good things you've got going on.

That's true happiness, if you ask me.

And although it's tempting to follow the crowd and chase short-term hits of dopamine over cultivating true happiness, I swear it's worth the fight. Because gratitude-induced well-being is the kind of happiness that has no "if" or "when." It's the kind that never goes out of style. It's the kind that, just like compassion, doesn't cost a dime.

Furthermore, gratitude is an act of rebellion on many levels.

It rebels against the gap.

It rebels against the "I'll-be-happy-when" syndrome.

It rebels against society's depiction of what happiness should look like.

It rebels against consumerism.

It rebels against misery, depression, and lack.

Gratitude creates magical results in our inner and outer worlds. But it's not magic.

It's science.

The Science of Gratitude

There have been hundreds upon hundreds of scientific studies carried out on gratitude, and for good reason. Gratitude is the human characteristic most widely associated with states of well-being. The more we study it, the more blown away scientists, brain experts, psychologists, and personal growth enthusiasts become. It's really powerful stuff.

My favorite study would probably be the one by Dr. Robert A. Emmons of the University of California, Davis. In this particular study, he asked all his participants to write a few sentences per week in their journals. The topic depended on which of three groups they were in.

The first group wrote about things they were grateful for.

The second group wrote about the things that went wrong or that displeased them in some way.

And the third group wrote about all the events that had affected them in the past week, with no particular emphasis on how positive or negative they were.

After ten weeks, the results came in. Unsurprisingly, those who focused on what they were grateful for felt more optimistic, fulfilled, and generally more positive about their lives. What was surprising, though, was that they also exercised more than usual and had fewer visits to doctors when compared to the other two groups. What's more, the effects *lasted* long after the experiment had finished.

As I said, this is one of the hundreds of incredible studies out there on the subject of gratitude. I imagine that you're not interested in trawling through every single one. But just know that all of them prove that when you create feelings of gratitude through thought alone, gratitude journaling, or meditation, incredibly interesting things start happening to your mind and body.

Here's what else scientific studies have proved to be true about gratitude. The benefits include:

1. Increased levels of energy and vitality
2. Higher emotional intelligence
3. Boosted mood (release of happy chemicals in the brain)
4. Greater tendency to forgive

5. Prevention or lessening of depression/anxiety
6. Improved relationships and sociability
7. Better, deeper sleep
8. Reduced inflammation/headaches
9. Less physical fatigue
10. Enhanced feelings of life satisfaction

A day in the life of the future you (with a regular gratitude practice) may look something like this, then. You wake up with the joys of spring after a deep, restorative sleep. You're ready to interact with your family and colleagues from the get-go thanks to your heightened emotional intelligence. You have a job that others may describe as stressful, but you don't feel it nearly as much as your colleagues do. You're not as fast to finger-point either. As you go through your daily meetings, your workmates often inquire as to why you seem so joyful all the time. You smile, feeling focused and vital in your body, as well as being totally ready for the challenges of the day. When you get home in the evening, you're still riding the waves of your good mood. And when you head to bed, you do so with a profound sense of satisfaction for another day well lived.

If someone offered us a little pill that provided all of these benefits, with no side effects, free of charge, we'd snatch their hand off, wouldn't we?

So why is it that we don't hear about gratitude, but we *do* hear about Prozac?

Well, the pharmaceutical lobby is massive. The gratitude lobby? Not so big.

Great for the mind, great for the pocket, gratitude doesn't require you to spend a single dime to be happy. All the deep healing and happiness is going to happen in your head. Organically. With no gluten. It also works just as well without a new salt lamp, yoga mat, grass-fed unsalted butter, prayer beads, or a *Discover Your Divine Feminine Through Aromatherapy* course book.

Okay, perhaps the one thing you'll want to buy yourself is a nice gratitude journal to write in before you go to bed. But that's it. You really do get more than you're required to put in with this one.

The Myths Behind Gratitude

Just as compassion is saddled with lots of misconceptions, gratitude also has its fair share of unhelpful myths. So let's break them down.

First off, a lot of people think that we can reap the benefits of gratitude only when things are going hunky-dory in our lives. And, granted, gratitude flows a lot easier when we're receiving gifts, eating gourmet food, getting paid, or painting the town red with our friends.

But if you ask me, gratitude shines the brightest in the darkest times. Gratitude in and of itself builds incredible levels of resilience and safeguards us from dropping into depressing rabbit holes. The ability to stop in the midst of pain and chaos and notice the value in it is a skill that will serve you until the day you die.

There will be times when you wake up in a foul mood due to a crappy night's sleep. But you have two choices: you can condemn yourself and your lack of shut-eye, or you can be grateful for the fact that, unlike at least one billion people in the world, you have a bed and a roof over your head.

I'm not belittling you and your feelings here. Lack of sleep sucks.

But we always have a choice as to where we direct our focus. Through this practice, you'll come to learn that no matter how grim things may seem, there's always something to be grateful for. And that makes navigating life's hardships a hell of a lot smoother.

Sure, a colleague was curt to you this morning, but can you be grateful for the fact that you have a well-paid job with other colleagues of the gentler type?

Sure, your last date ended pretty . . . badly, but can you be grateful that you never have to see them again and can enjoy the company of friends?

So, we're not denying our shortcomings here, we're just reframing them. We're extracting the gold from the dirt.

And there's always more gold in your life than you think.

Feeling grateful every day isn't dependent on huge wins like cashing in your lottery ticket, learning your book hit the *New York Times* bestseller list, or completing your first marathon. You can be just as grateful for the small things too.

Funnily enough, it doesn't particularly matter *what* you're appreciating; rather, it's how much you're *feeling* it.

Imagine being able to marinate in oxytocin and appreciation when you receive a hug from your kid.

Imagine experiencing pure elation when your coworker hands you a cup of tea as a treat.

Imagine taking your first conscious breath in the morning with a heart full of gratitude for the mere fact that you're alive.

It's not the size of the celebration that matters, it's the *motion of the emotion*.

So when you practice gratitude, try not to just speed through the mental motions like a checklist. Rather, feel into every single memory with all your senses. It's free, it's organic, and you deserve it.

And for those of you who have never actively participated in a regular gratitude practice, don't beat yourself up. It doesn't mean that you're an inherently ungrateful person. This is a gratitude *practice*, after all, and before you know it, it'll feel a lot more natural.

What's more, there may be people reading this book right now who have lived very tough lives. They may well be thinking that, during their lifetimes, they haven't received all that much to be grateful for. And that's fair. Oftentimes, the events in our lives come down to plain luck, and life can be a series of challenges and blocks.

But as I said before, one of the biggest myths about gratitude is that your life needs to be perfect in order for you to feel it.

If You're Going Through a Tough Time

Remember: Even the happiest people benefit from gratitude. But it's the unhappy people going through hell who *need* gratitude more than anyone else.

And that might be you right now.

Sometimes it seems like life hasn't dealt us a set of cards that are gratitude-worthy. You might not have been lucky enough to have it all be plain sailing.

Some of you reading this book right now are suffering in silence in an abusive relationship. Others may be stuck in a job where the working conditions are awful, governed by a company that violates their human rights. Some of you may be suffering from a debilitating illness.

In these incredibly trying times, I acknowledge that asking you to feel grateful for that particular hardship is a nearly impossible, borderline disrespectful, feat. So I'm not saying you should be in denial about your circumstances. Being grateful doesn't mean accepting an abusive relationship, putting up with a toxic work environment, or giving up the fight against cancer.

You can still be grateful for your life in general and simultaneously muster the strength to make the necessary changes to get yourself out of whichever painful situation you're in. And if you can, I urge you to do so.

There is always hope, no matter how faint.

You may have found this part hard to digest, which is completely understandable. But what I stick by is the fact that you can always, always show love and appreciation for one thing.

Yourself.

And you must. You deserve it more than I can describe.

This is called self-appreciation—and it's a fundamental part of the 6 Phase Meditation.

When you hit rock bottom, gratitude for the most simple things will be your saving grace.

Gratitude is the silent, unassuming key to surviving the biggest traumas as well as enjoying the pleasures of life. I could write a whole book about gratitude, but for now, I hope this chapter convinces you of its power and inspires you to get practicing.

The 3x3 Gratitude Method

Now that you know all about the science and benefits behind gratitude, as well as having smashed through the myths, I'll talk you through how we're going to approach the practice.

In the 6 Phase Meditation, I'll be taking you through the 3x3 Gratitude Method step by step. Again, you'll be fully guided by the audio, but it's good to gain some clarity on the process before you begin.

It's called the 3x3 Gratitude Method because you focus on three different aspects of your life and three things you're grateful for in each of these categories.

The three different aspects of your life are your personal life, your work life, and your fine self (aka—self-appreciation). Within each of those areas, you'll come up with three examples of things you're grateful for. For example:

PERSONAL LIFE

#1: I'm grateful that I get to wake up next to my amazing partner every single morning.

#2: I'm really appreciative of the fun, wine-drenched birthday party my friends threw for me last night.

#3: I'm truly grateful for the delicious cups of coffee my favorite café serves me each day.

WORK LIFE

#1: I'm grateful for my job and how challenging, stimulating, and fun it can be.

#2: I'm really appreciative of my colleague [insert colleague's name] and how they always give me a smile when I arrive at the office.

#3: I'm truly grateful for the money that flows to me from my company every single month—money that facilitates the high quality of life I live.

YOURSELF

#1: I'm grateful that I'm the type of person who finds it easy to give and receive affection, and I appreciate the fact that I am so lovable.

#2: I'm really appreciative of my body, and I love my shape.

#3: I'm truly grateful for my unique talents, the languages I speak, and my ability to use my mind to its maximum potential.

These are just some examples, but you can go wild here, as long as you cover all three bases.

I designed the exercise this way because what I kept noticing about gratitude meditators was that they tended to express gratitude only for the strongest area of their life.

If they were workaholics, they'd explore their professional wins and forget about their personal lives. If they were die-hard family people, they'd tend to focus only on their kids and spouses and forget about their careers. All this creates an imbalance.

Another mistake a lot of people make when they express gratitude is that they forget to feel grateful for themselves. Through our fear of being labeled narcissists, we seldom reflect on what makes us incredible. Because of this, we opt for getting our validation from external sources. We let other people fill our cups, latching on to feedback, compliments, and confirmation that we're good, successful people, as opposed to serving ourselves. So if you ask me, the problem isn't too much self-love but rather too little.

I don't know anyone who's hot on praising themselves, to be honest.

But I do know plenty of people who would be more than happy to share how unskilled they are, how their contribution to the world just isn't enough, or how much they detest the size of their thighs.

A Note on Body Image

This not-enoughness is most prevalent with body image. We've all got *something* against our poor bodies.

You may be overweight or underweight. You may be shorter or taller than "normal" for your gender. You may not have the enviable skin that television commercials say you should be proud of. You may have scars. You may have a visible health issue. You may have teeth that aren't sparkling white or straight. The list goes on, and odds are you'll deem yourself less than perfect in one of these areas.

But if you're reading this right now, you're a living, breathing human being who is here by complete, perfect fluke. You are the result of an obscenely lucky sperm that made it to one very lucky egg. You weren't just one in a million. You were one in *five hundred* million. Your body, the one that you're fortunate enough to inhabit, is a freakin' miracle in and of itself.

So, please, do yourself a favor and start appreciating your body as it is. We need to quit this whole thing about forcing our bodies into a particular stereotype of beauty.

We should take care of ourselves so we're healthy, sure, but enough with the shame.

What I've discovered is that when we train people to express gratitude for themselves and take a couple of minutes to reflect on everything they actually *like* about their bodies and their characters, great things start happening. Number one, it feels good, and that feeling of wholesomeness and peace travels with them all day.

Number two, they become less insecure, more confident, and more resilient to haters. They go from having holes to feeling whole.

Number three, their relationship with themselves gets much more solid.

Number four, their relationships with others get healthier because they're not as needy and reliant upon others' constant validation.

Not bad for a few seconds a day of self-appreciation, right?

Gratitude and Manifestation

If all these reasons to practice weren't enough—you know, the self-confidence, the happiness, the fewer visits to the doctors, the fulfillment, the saving grace from any pit of despair . . .

. . . There's actually more.

Gratitude has been strongly linked to achievement, success, and abundance.

Why? Because it's just like the much-loved motivational speaker "Zig" Ziglar once said:

The more you are grateful for what you have, the more you will have to be grateful for.

Some of the wealthiest people in the world have used gratitude as a practice to draw more money to them. And it works. In *The Science of Getting Rich*, author Wallace Wattles wrote:

The grateful mind is constantly fixed upon the best. Therefore, it tends to become the best; it takes the form or character of the best and will receive the best.

This isn't just fluff; it's logic. And if you land a regular gratitude practice, even if your bank balance doesn't change for a while, it'll feel like it has. Abundance is a mind-set, after all. And as we've seen, the abundant mind, just like a magnet, will draw more abundance to it. Like attracts like.

Try your best to perfect this gratitude practice; it may well be the single missing ingredient that's been keeping you from true joy, peace, and prosperity.

The Happiness and Gratitude Protocol

Step 1—Your Personal Life

First, you'll think about three things, events, or people from your personal life that you're grateful for.

It doesn't matter if you reflect on something from yesterday or from twenty years ago. It doesn't matter if a loved one is alive or deceased. It doesn't matter if it's a huge thing or a little thing. Feel free to mix and match topics and timelines—as long as you can feel the appreciation, it really doesn't matter.

You could reflect on the deep sleep you had last night that you really needed.

Perhaps you could appreciate your home and how it humbly shelters you from the cold and the rain.

You could bring to mind the delicious, nutritious food you have in your fridge—a privilege that billions will never experience.

You could remember the day you first clocked eyes on your spouse, relive the butterflies, and be thankful you met them.

Maybe you could appreciate that backpacking trip you took with friends when you were in your twenties, or any other precious memories that light you up when you think of them.

As I mentioned before, try not to just make a list. Because it's not about the list itself, but about the feelings associated with each memory, person, or thing. So feel the good vibes, feel the love, and embody the appreciation. This is the easy part. Step 2 can be a little more challenging for most.

Step 2—Your Work Life

Next, you'll shift your focus to what you're grateful for in your career and working life.

This was a very deliberate inclusion because many of us underestimate this area of our lives and the countless blessings that it brings us. But if we're spending five days of the week working, it makes sense that we ought to make work-based gratitude a habit.

Even if you thoroughly despise where you're at right now, there will be *something* you can be grateful for. I'm not saying you should stay there if you've been considering jumping out of the office block's window. If you're that unhappy, you probably should leave. But in the meantime, bring to mind three things about your work life that you value.

If nothing else, you could reflect on how grateful you are for that cash that appears in your account every single month, and how it supports you and your family.

You could bring to mind a special colleague you work with and feel thankful for the kindness they have shown you.

You might be thankful for the sky-high demands of your job, and how they've facilitated your learning and growth.

You could even reminisce over that crazy Christmas party you had a few years back when the receptionist got drunk and dove into *way* too much detail about her nonexistent sex life . . . and feel happy you got to witness the hilarious awkwardness of it all.

Just watch that space. Before you know it, you'll have shifted your perspective on your job for the better, and feel so much more positive for it.

Step 3—Yourself

Okay, so for the newbies to personal growth and inner inquiry, this will probably feel difficult at first.

Like I said earlier, step 3 is all about honoring and respecting something that we've never been taught to honor or respect . . . ourselves.

And when you start loving yourself through a self-gratitude practice, you can then head out into the world as the best, most confident version of yourself.

So just like in steps 1 and 2, you're going to pick three focal points.

Maybe you start by appreciating your openness to give this a go in the first place, which in and of itself sets you apart from a lot of people.

Perhaps you feel grateful that you're a kind person, with a good heart.

You could pick out a physical aspect of yourself you appreciate having, like the color of your eyes, your strong legs that have carried you around the world, or your authentic smile that makes other people smile too.

You could reflect on your intellectual feats, such as how much you appreciate your mind for constantly expanding, learning new languages or skills, and coming up with fresh ideas.

Maybe you could thank yourself for your motivation, for how you never miss a yoga session, for how you (almost) always hit your deadlines and strive to eat healthily every day.

You could thank yourself for being a great father, or reflect on how far you've come as a businesswoman.

Go for it. This last step is the most difficult but by far the most important. When all else fails, and the cards you get dealt in your personal and professional life bring you to your knees, you can always fall back on self-appreciation.

So, here we are, reversing the effects of the "I'll-be-happy-when" syndrome.

We're reversing that forward gap.

We're taking the reins of our mental health without the need for a pricey prescription.

The time you spend in a state of gratitude is never, ever wasted. And as we've seen, there's always something to be grateful for. It goes without saying that we live in an imperfect world, and there will always be changes we wish to see in our lives and the lives of others. The "I'll-be-happy-when" syndrome will always be a tempting path to follow, but we aren't going to tread it.

Because now we know that the only antidote to our unending cycles of desire, yearning, emptiness, and striving is gratitude. Stocking up on it is the smartest thing we can do if we want to live a truly happy life. Period.

The famous Greek Stoic philosopher Epictetus summed it up best a couple of thousand years ago. And his words are as true today as they were then.

> *He is a wise man who does not grieve for the things which he has not, but rejoices for those which he has.*

Before you proceed to the next chapter, open up your Mindvalley app and launch the 6 Phase Meditation program. From there, you can jump into the full interactive lesson for Phase 2: Happiness and Gratitude. The lesson is just a few minutes long and will recap some of the most important points in this chapter.

Upon completion, you can then dive straight into the meditation audio where I'll guide you through the gratitude protocol. It will take less than five minutes but will help lock in the second phase of your practice. As we progress we will layer on each phase. So in this audio we will start with Phase 1: The Circle of Love and Compassion and then stack on Phase 2: Happiness and Gratitude. This stacking causes each phase to build upon the one before, thus enhancing the potency of the meditation.

CHAPTER 3

PHASE 3

Peace Through Forgiveness

*As I walked out the door towards the gate that
would lead to my freedom, I knew that if I didn't leave
my bitterness and hatred behind, I'd still be in prison.*

NELSON MANDELA

Allow me to introduce you to the three Rs: resentment, rejection, and regret.

As a human being living on planet Earth, you'll experience all three at some point or another.

These babies, above all other feelings, are the most insidious. They're the ones that linger and eat away at your state of mind for days, weeks, months, and even years.

The reason? They're all based on events that happened in the past.

And just like the world's favorite shamanic monkey says in Disney's *The Lion King*:

Oh, yes, the past can hurt!

As Rafiki whacks Simba on the head relentlessly with his crooked staff, Simba comes to realize that just because something hurtful happened in the past, that doesn't mean the pain has gone anywhere. And unless we learn something from it and let it go, the three Rs will continue to stay. The whacks and wallops of life will continue to rain down on our heads, feeling harder and harder to bear.

That's where forgiveness comes in.

Forgiveness: The Ultimate Antidote for the Pains of Your Past

A widely accepted definition of forgiveness goes as follows:

Forgiveness is the decision to let go of the desire for revenge and ill will toward the person who wronged you.

I agree, but I think it's more than that. I think that forgiveness is less about the other person and more about setting yourself free from negativity. I believe that forgiveness is the underrated antidote to the poison that comes from the three Rs. Because you can't change the past, but you *can* reframe the way you think about it.

It's through forgiveness that the burn of anger, upset, and hostility can cool off, making room for happiness again.

It's through forgiveness that our hearts and relationships can heal.

It's through forgiveness that we can walk forward into a brighter future, free from the chains of *he/she/them-who-must-not-be-named*. More on that later.

Furthermore, science is now discovering some pretty mind-blowing news about how forgiveness affects your physical body.

The Weird, Incredible Benefits of Forgiving

A co-study by various universities in America, Asia, and Europe found out that "people induced to feel forgiveness perceive hills to be less steep and jump higher in ostensible fitness tests than people who are induced to feel unforgiveness."

These findings proved that forgiveness can literally lighten the physical burden of unforgiveness, facilitating better health, perfor-mance, and stamina.

The benefits of forgiveness don't just stop at feeling a bit lighter emotionally . . . forgiveness can literally make your *body weight* feel lighter while hiking up a mountain or shooting hoops.

Good news for sherpas and NBA players, then.

No joke, after I was lecturing on this forgiveness study one time, I actually had an Olympian basketball player contact me. He wanted to know how to go deeper with forgiveness meditations so he could go for gold on his jumps.

Here's another unexpected, odd benefit. For those of you with cardiovascular issues, listen up. Forgiveness has also been proven to support a healthy heart rate as well as improve blood pressure. Isn't that beautiful? The physical *and* the metaphorical hearts are healed by forgiveness—two birds with one stone.

Additionally, when you've worked on forgiveness, you're way less likely to have compromised mental health and taken that bad juju out on those around you. So when you make the decision to forgive, the ripple effects of hurt end with you.

That's pretty heroic, right?

Who'd have thought that all these advantages could be birthed from short, meditation-based forgiveness exercises?

All this revolutionary forgiveness stuff is relatively new to me, by the way. Forgiving whoever wronged me was never my forte. Not by a long shot. I actually came across the benefits of forgiving our enemies by a lucky accident.

And this is where the story gets a little more metaphysical.

An Experiment to Biohack a Monk's Brain Activity onto Our Own

It all started when I got myself strapped up in a dark room in British Columbia, twelve electrodes stuck to my head, hoping I could zen out under pressure.

It was 2016, and I was in one of the strangest establishments I'd ever been in. I was about to experience the physical, mental, and, more important, spiritual benefits of forgiveness firsthand.

But I can assure you I wasn't expecting any of it.

I'd decided to enroll in a five-day brain-training experience called 40 Years of Zen. It was a joint event by Dr. James Hardt and famed biohacker Dave Asprey. I did so with the hopes of rewiring my mind through meditation in order to "tap into my unlocked potential." I wasn't 100 percent clear on what that meant, which is partially the reason I turned up. I'm a sucker for a mystery.

It set me back fifteen *thousand* dollars to make it onto the waiting list. Fifteen thousand dollars was no joke. It goes without saying that the classes and experiments I participated in were filled with high-flying, very successful, very wealthy individuals, all hoping to over-dose on bliss. Little did we know that it was forgiveness that would get us there.

Long before my arrival, the scientists at the institute had been hard at work studying the brain-wave states of Zen monks who'd spent twenty to forty years deep in meditative practices.

As they analyzed the results, they noticed something very differ-ent about the monks' brains compared to the average Joe's brain. Specifically, two things. First, their alpha levels (the waves your brain emits when you're relaxed) had seriously high wave amplitudes. Sec-ond, the brain waves had what is known as "left-right brain coher-ence" (an impressive brain-wave symmetry between the logical, analytical side and the creative, intuitive side). And all this was true not just while they were meditating but also in their normal, every-day waking state.

The entire team was excited about these findings and explained to us how alpha-wave-inducing meditation can change your brain for the better, help you get into flow, bump up your IQ, and even in-crease your creativity.

But more exciting still, they informed the new batch of science guinea pigs, the batch I was part of, that they were looking into whether it was possible to transfer Zen-like states of mind to normal people. They were seeking to create permanent shifts in one's brain patterns to resemble the brains of monks who had been consistently meditating for twenty to forty years.

Here's where my ears well and truly pricked up.

I soon came to realize that this stuff isn't hokey, it's *real*. Thanks to my inherent skepticism, my tolerance for fluff was and continues to be pretty low. Show me the science and it's a done deal. And at that institute, you got nothing but experiments, analyses, and results.

Each day for five days, after the five hours of meditation in a chamber with our brains hooked up to machines, we would sit with our dedicated neuroscientist and analyze our brain-wave states and changes.

I had been under the impression that I knew all there was to know about the key elements of meditation and how to use them for maximum results.

But I was wrong.

Although my brain waves reflected a pretty zenned-out state of mind, my results were nothing when compared to Sally's.

It was Sally who planted the seeds of curiosity about forgiveness. It was Sally who inspired Phase 3.

Sally, without a shadow of a doubt, had one of the biggest brain-wave transformations the institute had ever seen. Her story was the stuff of legend. Sally had come to the institute desperate and stressed out. But over the five days, her brain waves showed remarkable improvements that gobsmacked the scientists there.

But what exactly was she doing to get such amazing results?

At this point, the institute was still in its early years and the researchers weren't yet completely sure about which meditative modalities would lead to these blissed-out states. It was the calmest free-for-all ever. They'd simply set people up in biofeedback chambers and tell them to go crazy. Relax, deep breathe, think happy thoughts, visualize the ocean, figure it out.

So that's what Sally did. But her progress was second to none.

When the institute inquired about what technique she was using, she asked, "You really want to know?"

They really did. The board of scientists nodded in sync and witnessed her take a deep breath in before exclaiming shamelessly:

I was forgiving the hell out of my asshole husband.

Sally went on to explain that she had dedicated herself to actively forgiving her ex-husband throughout her brain training sessions. To this day we still have no idea what her ex-husband did to her. But whatever steam she was letting out of her system as she meditated in the lab was working wonders for her brain.

Forgiveness as an alpha-wave-inducing megatool? Interesting. Turns out, after studying thousands upon thousands of people from all walks of life, the scientists at the institute claim that there's one surefire way to attain these desirable brain states. And that's through a forgiveness practice. Forgiveness was the key to getting one's brain waves to most closely resemble those of Zen-Roshi monks who had spent decades meditating.

But here's where the concept got kind of spooky.

On day four of the event, I'd sat down for breakfast at an inn nearby where I was lodging with fellow participants. Suddenly we saw Matt (name changed) running down the stairs, looking at his phone.

Now Matt had joined us at the institute because he'd been going through a tough time. Exactly why, before that morning, he'd not chosen to share. Visibly perturbed, he looked like he'd just seen a ghost.

"Matt, what's the matter?" I asked.

Matt replied, "My . . . my brother just messaged me."

"Was it bad news, did something go wrong?"

"No . . . It's just that I haven't spoken to my brother in two years."

Matt went on to explain that something inexplicable had just happened. You see, Matt had spent the last three days at the institute forgiving his brother. And what his brother had done to him when he was a child had really messed him up.

In his twenties, Matt had become severely addicted to cocaine and sex with prostitutes to deal with the pain. His unhealthy relationship with intimacy was ruining his life, as he felt unable to create meaningful relationships. But it wasn't the cliché fame-got-to-him story. He wasn't living the rock-and-roll, live-fast-die-young lifestyle out of jovial vigor.

He'd found himself on the road to ruin because his brother had abused him sexually when he was a child.

Needless to say, Matt loathed his brother.

At the institute, upon learning about the power of forgiveness for personal healing, he'd spent time attempting to forgive his brother. And that's when, on day four, something quite unusual happened. Matt's brother, out of the blue, had sent him a video on his phone telling Matt how sorry he was, asking for forgiveness himself.

Matt's brother had absolutely no idea that he was at this institute.

His story shocked all of us.

This showed that forgiveness seemed to cross some nonphysical boundaries and impact the lives of the people we are seeking to forgive. Furthermore, forgiveness had a way of healing both the victim and the perpetrator.

Forgiveness: Ripple Effects in the Nonphysical Field

Years later, I came across an idea that explains phenomena like this in an interview I did with Gary Zukav, an American self-empowerment teacher and author. He spoke about how utterly and deeply connected we are to one another in the nonphysical world—much more than we've been taught to believe.

Here's what Gary told me:

The nonphysical law allows you to use nonphysical causes to create nonphysical effects and also physical effects. This does not mean that you are not in control of what you create. On the contrary! It means that you are entirely free to create what you want, provided you are aware of how the nonphysical law of cause and effect works.

So Gary would say that what happened with Matt was no coincidence. Matt created that outcome with his brother in the nonphysical field via forgiveness.

Gary went on to explain that nonphysical reality is actually more our home than the physical reality we're seeing around us right now. If you think about it, we came from nonphysical reality before we were born, and we'll return to it when we die. But while we live on Earth, a huge part of us still resides and evolves within that nonphysical realm. Therefore, the majority of our interactions with other human beings may actually be occurring in that same nonphysical reality. Gary put it this way:

> *Your intentions are your nonphysical causes that set energy into motion. They create a multitude of effects and, therefore, determine the experiences of your life.*

It's become apparent that, even if the other person doesn't know you're forgiving them for something, the act, in and of itself, can create ripples none of us currently understand. Apart from feeling good in our own system, then, could forgiveness directly affect and influence the behavior of those around you? The simple answer is yes.

So I decided to try it myself.

My Strange Stroke of Luck After Experiencing Deep Forgiveness

After doing some of my own research on a few of the other benefits, I felt drawn to give this forgiveness thing a try myself. And funnily enough, the day I decided to forgive my biggest pain point, I managed to hit my highest levels of alpha-wave amplitude to date.

I remember opening my eyes after the meditation was over, tears streaming down my cheeks, before being greeted by the highest number I've ever scored on the biofeedback screen. It was a sight for sore eyes (literally).

But the good stuff didn't stop there. In the summer of 2017, I returned to my forgiveness training at 40 Years of Zen, this time in Seattle. There it was confirmed that forgiveness not only increases your peace of mind and alpha levels but also creates magical results in your outer world.

The scientists there explained to me that one of the side effects of going deep into this process is that synchronicity and manifesting accelerate. In short, your innermost desires and dreams come true faster and more easily. But being scientists, they didn't use the words *synchronicity* or *manifesting*. Instead, what they said is that people seemed to get "luckier."

What a beautiful promise.

Now, like 99 percent of children in my generation, I had been told by older and wiser humans that if something sounds too good to be true it probably is. So I went in there with my doubts. What happened next was a bit of really outlandish, unexpected, mind-blowing *luck*.

After I'd finished all my forgiveness training that summer, I returned home and went about my life. I returned to the "real" world—you know, work, kids, bills, normal stuff. I'd forgotten about what the scientists said about the whole forgiveness-induced-happily-ever-after thing.

The year before I'd just published my first book *The Code of the Extraordinary Mind*. To be honest, I was a little anxious about how it was going. When you write a book, you automatically put yourself in a very vulnerable spot. The urge to search for reviews and rankings is overwhelmingly strong, but you don't. You don't, because you'd become obsessed. It's a slippery slope. So it's a rule. Once you publish a book, your only job is to let go of the results and hope for the best.

By that point, I knew it had become moderately successful, but even so, you never, *ever* snoop around your Amazon page or glance at your book sales or rankings. You tell yourself you're done and you move on to your next book.

A few weeks after my training I had a weird impulse. "Check your book on Amazon," said my intuition one afternoon as I was working at my computer. (Side note—when you practice forgiveness, you become more intuitive.)

What? No. I wouldn't. You DO NOT check the Amazon page.

"Check your book on Amazon."

But . . .

"Check your book on Amazon."

That voice was pretty persistent that I should break the rules this time.

I caved.

What the hell? I checked again. It can't be. I checked again.

Amazon was showing me as the second best-selling author in the world, ahead of Tolkien and J. K. Rowling. And weirder still, the day before, on September 16, 2017, my book had become the number one book *in the world* on Amazon Kindle.

Now that, for me as a writer, was music to my disbelieving ears.

Was this a coincidence? Maybe. Or was it the "luck" those scientists had spoken about?

Forgiveness, it turns out, is a transcendental training in and of itself that can lead to extraordinary events in our lives. It's an incredibly powerful manifestation tool as well as a path to health and prosperity.

Do we fully understand it? No. But as physicist Nassim Haramein once said, "Spirituality is nothing more than physics that we have yet to find an equation for."

But . . . Can We Forgive Anything and Anyone?

I know what you're thinking. All this is well and good, but what if someone did something really, really bad?

What if the act is unforgivable?

First of all, at the end of the day, you're doing it for you, not for them. Not forgiving is cheating yourself because you, of course, are worthy of all these benefits and deserve to live a life without resentment.

The first rule of forgiveness is that we absolutely can forgive *anything.*

Just think about my friend Matt the next time you think something is unforgivable. If Matt can forgive his brother for sexually abusing him when he was a child, you can forgive whoever hurt you. If Nelson Mandela can invite his jailers (who locked him up unjustly for twenty-seven years) over for dinner to break bread, you can forgive whoever it is that messed up your life.

Forgiveness liberates you, but as we've seen, it can also open doors to amazing opportunities and provide you with the traits you need to live your best life.

How Forgiveness Frees You: Ken Honda's Story

There's this incredible man by the name of Ken Honda. He's also known as "the happy panda" and happens to be Japan's pride and joy. And for good reason.

The "Zen Millionaire" (another name he goes by) is truly one of the most successful, nicest, and most fulfilled people I've ever met. And guess what? He attributes his success, in large part, to the practice of forgiveness.

In his Mindvalley *Money EQ* course, he shared something quite personal with us.

When Ken was a little boy, he was scared to be around his father. As an extremely regimented, struggling Japanese businessman, his father had been hardened by life's challenges and tended to take it out on his son. But Ken's father never told him what problems he was carrying, and he never, ever strayed from the stoic path. Like most Japanese men at the time, his father would never show his emotions.

That is, until one evening when Ken wandered into the kitchen to find his father sobbing.

Seeing his father's face reddened and huge tears streaming into the manly hands that attempted to shield his face, Ken witnessed something he'd never seen before.

He didn't know it was possible for a man to cry.

"My father . . . crying?"

Needless to say, Ken was taken aback. What could have caused his big, authoritative, rock of a father to cry like a baby?

The one thing that made the world go round. Money.

That was the beginning of a downward spiral. They were struggling financially, and at that tender age, Ken became very aware of their money issues.

Money must be bad.

Money is stressful.

There's never enough money.

Money makes my dad cry.

These, among others, were the beliefs Ken absorbed about the concept of money. They're classic.

Our limiting beliefs are given to us by our parents, and they quickly turn into huge blocks that solidify over time. Money blocks are probably the most common of all, but unfortunately, they often have the biggest consequences. One of the consequences? Money stops flowing to you because *you don't believe* it will. It caused Ken a lot of difficulties as he grew up, and it was all his dad's fault.

Not only had his father abandoned him emotionally and shown him little to no love growing up, but he'd also bestowed huge money blocks on him. Thanks a lot, Dad.

That said, there's a happy ending to the story. Judging by Ken's profile today, it goes without saying that he found a way to rise above it all. How? Ken describes what happened:

The most important thing for me to do was to forgive my father. After a few tries, I finally forgave him. And in this forgiveness, we found such a deep connection. I even heard him say the words, "I'm sorry for everything." I wasn't expecting that.

Ken forgave him for giving him such a hard time when he was a child, and it turned out that Ken's father had been treated the exact same way by his own father.

He was hurt a long time before me in the same way by his father. So now we have a new connection. Empathy. Today we have made such a deep bonding as brothers.

Hurt people hurt people, after all, and that understanding helped Ken bond with his father and accelerate the forgiveness. But that wasn't all. Not only did Ken heal his money wounds, but the newfound empathy he had for his father opened the door to his huge success story. Here's what Ken told me:

I used to have a lot of issues listening to people who were older than me because I didn't trust them like I didn't trust my father. But after healing all this hurt with my father, I was able to become closer to older people. That's why I became such a good student with many of my money mentors, including the great Wahei Takeda.

It was Wahei Takeda, the Warren Buffett of Japan, who mentored Ken into becoming Japan's number one writer of fifty-plus books. One in twenty Japanese people have read Ken. No other writer even comes close. And it's thanks to his own forgiveness journey that he's been able to help millions of people heal their money wounds for a better life too.

"I Have Sent You Nothing but Angels"

Any Neale Donald Walsch fans out there will know that he too is a huge advocate for forgiveness. He's mostly known for his *Conversations with God* book series (which have sold more than fifteen million copies). But as amazing as those books are, it's one of his lesser-known works that has a really special place in my heart. It's a children's book about forgiveness.

By the way, if, like me, you have young kids and are interested in teaching them how to forgive and healthily navigate all the emotions that come with it, you definitely want to grab a copy. It's called *The Little Soul and the Sun*. In that book, Neale shares a very interesting message: in short, that God, the Great Spirit, the universe, sends you whatever you need (not what you want) at the right time.

If someone betrays you, although you may deem them to be the devil in disguise, they're actually there to teach you valuable lessons and provide you with an opportunity for self-discovery. As God says to the Little Soul in the book, "I have sent you nothing but angels."

That's not to say you have to be best buddies with the perpetrator. That's a common misconception about forgiveness, and it tends to put people off. Forgiveness is not about getting back with your ex or dropping the charge if someone has committed a criminal offense against you. It's not a pardon, and it doesn't justify the horrible, heinous acts that you may have suffered through. No way. Leave that to the legal system.

In short, you can forgive the thief. But you still report him to the law so he doesn't go on to rob someone else.

Even if you didn't press charges, at the very least you can rest in the knowledge that karma's a bitch.

Joking.

(Not.)

But on a serious note, hear me when I say that forgiveness is never about the other person. Forgiveness is a personal, internal process of healing. It's all about *you* and your well-being, not about anyone else's.

You're doing this for *yourself*, not for them.

Through this process of letting go, you're wisely liberating yourself from the poisonous three Rs (resentment, rejection, and regret, remember?) and deciding to leave the rest up to the universe.

What's more, Neale advocates the idea that, once you're literate in forgiveness, you'll get to a place where you'll actually have fewer and fewer things to forgive in the first place.

"The master never needs to forgive," he told me, "for the master understands."

Neale explained to me that at a certain point, after truly, deeply going into forgiveness, the act eventually becomes automatic. At that point, you simply understand the perspectives of others (however flawed) and are no longer triggered by their bad decisions or actions.

This is the key to the next idea: becoming *unf*ckwithable*.

Forgiveness: A Fast Track to Unf*ckwithability

That's another thing forgiveness gives you. The ability to be calm and powerful in the face of attack.

I remember traveling to the airport after my experience at the 40

Years of Zen event. The participants in the class had gotten so close we had all decided to stay in touch with one another online.

As I was being driven to the airport I saw that Matt had posted a message in our group chat.

It was a meme that read like this:

UNF*CKWITHABLE
DEFINITION—(adj.) When you're truly at peace and in touch with yourself, and nothing anyone says or does bothers you, and no negativity or drama can touch you.

Matt wrote below the image. "I think all this forgiveness just made us all unf*ckwithable!"

I smiled. And I fully agreed.

Unf*ckwithable people don't just happen. Badass people are grown from turbulent life experiences, grit, blood, sweat, tears, and hard-core forgiveness of the highest caliber.

So that's what forgiveness gives you as a parting gift, along with milestone life lessons. But when I refer to forgiveness, I'm not just referring to the perpetrators who graced your life with their bullsh*t. There's self-forgiveness to tackle too. That's another ball game.

Do You Need to Forgive Yourself?

Self-forgiveness is even more hard-core.

Many of us carry secret regrets and self-loathing around with us like rocks in our pockets without even knowing it. But as time goes by, that missing forgiveness will have a huge impact on your self-esteem.

Listen. If you've done wrong, learned your lesson, and are committed to not doing it again, you deserve your own forgiveness. Period.

You can let it go. We all screw up, and that doesn't make us bad people. Our mistakes don't have to define us. Our ugly acts don't make us inherently ugly. Just remember: The best apology to anyone else and yourself is *changed behavior*.

As you read the forgiveness protocol, know that it is there to help you forgive yourself too.

Once you get good at it, you can remove those tiny pocket rocks or huge boulders of resentment out of your metaphorical backpack. Whether it's shaking off the shade your waiter threw at you at last night's dinner, forgiving yourself for a huge betrayal, or cleansing yourself of the pinpricks of grudges against those you love, the benefits of forgiving are endless.

Again, you're not pardoning anyone or doing this for anyone other than yourself. Remember this.

Without further ado, here's the forgiveness protocol I designed for the 6 Phase. It's inspired by Dr. James Hardt and refined by Dave Asprey's team at 40 Years of Zen.

So be kind to yourself, go slow, and allow your forgiveness skills to deepen over time.

The Forgiveness Protocol

Step 1—Identify the Person or Act to Forgive

Choose the person or act that you'd like to forgive.

If you're doing this for the first time, start with something small. Forgiveness is like a muscle; you need to strengthen it before delving into the heavy stuff. I'd pick a person I genuinely loved, like my partner or my kid, and forgive them for an everyday annoyance of some kind. From there, with practice, you can build it up to the more major, traumatic events that have haunted you for years. But not just yet.

Remember, you can also choose to forgive a younger version of yourself for something you did in the past. This can be just as transformative, if not more so, as forgiving someone else.

Step 2—Create the Space

Pick a comforting, relaxing environment in your mind to allow the forgiveness process to happen.

You can choose a real place, like your garden or living room, or you can imagine a place—say, on a tropical Costa Rican beach. It could even be your version of heaven or a holy place of worship. Bring that person to mind and see them standing in front of you in this environment. Know that you're protected and nothing bad can happen on this mental, theatrical stage. This is all happening in the safety of your mind.

Step 3—Read the Charge

Imagine inviting the person, or representation of the act, into your safe space. You're about to read out the charge as though you were a judge in court.

For example, you could recite the misdeeds like this: "[insert name], you brought me pain and suffering by [insert misdeed]."

Keep it formal, professional, and detached, but try your best to cover the details too. Read it like you're a professional attorney speaking in court. Say it all, including why you think the misdeed was so wrong. Leave nothing out.

Here is an example of a charge I mentally read out when I was forgiving a former school principal for punishing me cruelly when I was a kid.

I had forgotten my shorts for PE class that day. And you wanted to exploit your power, so you picked on me. I was fourteen years old. I was a kid. My only mistake was forgetting to pack my shorts. Yet you made me stand in the hot sun on the basketball court for three hours. My class teacher asked you to stop. I was a good student and had great grades. I sweated in the sun till I almost fainted. I lost my respect for you. I lost my respect for my school. The punishment must fit the crime. You cannot punish a young kid like that.

Step 4—Feel the Anger and Pain

After stating the charge, take a moment to fully feel the anger, resentment, and sadness this person may have caused you.

Allow yourself to express it too—shout, scream, cry, curse, whatever you need to do to bring all these feelings to a climax. (Don't worry, this will only aggravate your pain temporarily. Think about it like a clenched fist—you have to clench it fully to then completely release and relax it.) You can set a timer for two minutes if that feels safer. Afterward, take a deep breath in and choose to let it all go.

The goal here is to not bury your feelings. It's to let them out and then heal them.

Step 5—Identify the Lessons You Learned

Rumi said, "The wound is the place where the light enters"—meaning, there is value to be claimed from every seemingly negative experience. So what did you learn from this scenario?

For example, "From this painful experience, I learned to set healthy boundaries and break my addiction to people-pleasing," or "I learned that I'm so much stronger and more resilient than I gave myself credit for."

When we identify the lessons in our hardships that made us better people, we give meaning to our suffering. That step reframes it and gives it worth, laying the foundation for us to move forward, cleansed of resentment. My friend Michael Beckwith refers to this as a "kensho" moment, translating as "growth through pain."

Step 6—Think of How the Other Person May Have Been Hurt in the Past

Hurt people hurt people. So how did this person suffer in the past? What happened to facilitate their bad behavior toward you?

For example, in my case, "[insert name] hurt me in this way because of his own lack of self-esteem, which he's had since childhood, when he suffered bullying at school. It was self-sabotage."

Let your ideas flow freely. People are very rarely inherently evil, and considering their story will help you put the pieces together and form a logical understanding.

If this part doesn't come easy, it might help to transform the person in your mind's eye to their younger self. See them standing there as a child. What could have screwed them up so badly that they felt that this behavior was okay?

When I thought about the school principal who punished me so cruelly as a kid, I remembered that he was a former weight lifter. Perhaps he had a coach who pushed him too far. Perhaps he felt that he was making me stronger by pushing me in turn. When I saw him as a younger man, perhaps with an abusive coach, I began to understand where his strictness came from.

Step 7—See the Scene Through Their Eyes

For this step, you'll need to imagine you have mind-reading superpowers. Imagine you're floating out of your body straight into theirs. See the scenario through their eyes.

What might their thought process have been to explain why they did what they did to you? How did they feel as they were doing it? Did they even consider that their actions might cause you pain? How did they see you at the time?

Again, it helps greatly to imagine them as a child. What did they witness or experience that might have caused them to act in this way as a flawed adult?

You don't have to justify it or agree with it by any stretch of the imagination, just experience it for yourself as best you can. This is where empathy comes in and separation fizzles out. We're all humans, we're all connected, and we're all flawed in some way.

Step 8—Forgive into Love

I know this step may seem corny, but it's very deliberate. When I asked the scientists at the Biocybernaut Institute how we'd know if we'd truly forgiven someone, they said: "It's hard to tell, but the best measure of it would be a hug. If you saw that person in your mind in front of you while you're meditating and felt at ease with the idea of hugging them, you've most likely forgiven them into love."

So ask yourself if you can visualize forgiving this person in your safe space with love to the point of hugging them. If you're struggling, it can help to visualize them as a child again, a lost innocent child who didn't know any better. So hug them, safe in the knowledge that you're absolutely protected. By this stage, you should be feeling a lot lighter.

Now, you've healed yourself, not them. You've removed a potentially huge, karmic scar from your system. If we were to measure your brain waves now, we'd see a dramatic increase in your alpha waves and left-right brain coherence.

If you have something really painful to heal, you might have the same person in your daily Phase 3 for the next few weeks. But you can rest assured that you will forgive them in time. You get out what you put in. And if your intention is pure, if your true desire is to forgive, you'll achieve it. Trust me.

I'm not saying this process is easy. It's not meant to be.

And I'll put it out there here and now that this is by far the most challenging of all the phases of the 6 Phase Meditation. It takes a lot of strength to do this, and most people never even bother trying. But now you know why it's worth your while to be the bigger person who does. Now you know that it's forgiveness that liberates you from the pain that holds you back from the best version of yourself.

As Rumi once said, "Oh ye who can't take a good rub. How will you ever become a polished gem?"

So, allow yourself to get buffed by the roughness of life, with all the flawed and fallible humans who surround you on the journey.

Because then, and only then, can you go out there and shine for all the world to see.

Before you proceed to the next chapter, open up your Mindvalley app and launch the 6 Phase Meditation program. From there, you can jump into the full interactive lesson for Phase 3: Peace Through Forgiveness. The lesson is just a few minutes long and will recap some of the most important points in this chapter. Upon completion, you can then dive straight into the meditation audio where I'll guide you through the forgiveness protocol. It will take less than five minutes but will help lock in the third phase of your practice.

Bonus: In the 6 Phase Meditation course that comes with this book, I've also included a bonus video where I teach an intuition-based technique to help you gauge if and when you're done forgiving someone. That way, you'll know when to move on to the next item on your forgiveness list.

CHAPTER 4

PHASE 4

A Vision for Your Future

All we have to decide is what to do with the time that is given to us.

GANDALF, *LORD OF THE RINGS*

I had a dream.

Sure, it wasn't Martin Luther King–level, but it was a pretty grandiose goal to me.

I, Vishen Lakhiani, wanted to represent my country, Malaysia, in a world-class international Taekwondo tournament.

It was 1993, and I was seventeen years old. At the time I was really into martial arts, worshipping my ultimate deities: Bruce Lee and Jean-Claude Van Damme (who at that time had just starred in the movie *Kickboxer*). I was the type of kid who could barely maintain a conversation at school—and since I'd been picked on most of my life, my father, like any good dad, had decided to enroll me in Taekwondo (also known as Korean karate) so I could kick butt.

Since it bestowed a newfound sense of self-confidence on me, Taekwondo quickly became my obsession. I would practice in the garden every single day, kicking our papaya tree barefoot, just like Jean-Claude Van Damme would in his iconic role in *Kickboxer*. I, of course, never managed to topple that papaya tree, and I usually gave up at the first sign of stabbing pain, but my enthusiasm was undeniable.

But this one afternoon my martial arts instructor told me the most exciting news of my life thus far: that there was going to be a major Taekwondo competition at the US Open 1993 in Colorado later that year, and that I had a shot at representing our flag.

First, I'd have to beat all of my classmates in a wood-breaking competition. Then, after getting selected, I'd compete against all the other top players in my country at the nationals. If I landed gold in both, I had a chance of being selected to play in the US Open.

I'd never set foot in the United States before and it would be an understatement to say that it was my ultimate dream to go. The USA was a mecca for me. I'd often catch myself daydreaming about what it would be like: the land of Hollywood movie stars, MTV, Coca-Cola, hamburgers . . .

To add to the allure, my instructor told us he'd throw in a trip to Disneyland for the finalists.

So that settled it. I *had* to win this competition. And it soon became the biggest obsession of my seventeen-year-old brain.

While my peers focused their attention on girls and video games, I went about furthering my studies on the philosophies of creative visualization. Back then, I was an avid manifestation geek.

My obsession with meditation and creative visualization had started when I discovered a book called *The Silva Mind Control Method* on my father's bookshelf. The author, José Silva—who I mentioned earlier—had developed a powerful method to train your brain to enter relaxed states before visualizing the outcomes you wanted.

The Silva Method was one of America's earliest and most popular personal growth programs and it was as big in the 1980s as Tony Robbins or Mindvalley is today.

Arming myself with my basic knowledge of the Silva Method, I went about practicing. I became quite the teen connoisseur of creative visualization. Around ten months before the competition, I'd sit down three times a day, every day, to see my dream unfold. I saw it all. I saw myself landing in the United States and breathing in American air, which I assumed was filled with awesomeness and can-do. I saw myself heading to the training center in my badass Taekwondo uniform. I saw those flashing lights bathing me in attention, applause surrounding me, as I marched into the ring to face my opponent, "MALAYSIA" sewn with love on the back of my perfectly ironed Taekwondo uniform.

The day finally came. It was time to literally smash stage one: the wood-breaking competition. At this stage, you'd find yourself facing three human beings with black belts holding three planks of wood. The rules were simple: break all three pieces of two-inch-thick planks they were holding with one kick, in the fastest time possible.

I'd be up against my fellow classmates, my friends. But they were no friends of mine today. Today, I'd have no mercy. Disneyland was at stake.

I heard the whistle blow.

I took a deep breath. I knew I had a few seconds to break every single piece, and I was as ready as I ever would be. I lifted my foot gracefully in what felt like slow motion and let out my best imitation of a high-pitch kung fu–style *heia!*

BOOM.

BOOM.

BOOM.

Done. I put down my foot like a ninja, and the wood was still there intact. But that didn't faze me one bit. I was confident it would break. It would be like one of those epic scenes from a samurai movie where the warrior would slice his enemy in two, only to see the pieces slide apart seconds later in slow motion.

Once they did, the pieces would fall to the ground, and I'd marinate joyfully in rapturous applause.

Ten seconds later, the wood was still solid.

The whistle blew again.

I was out.

I'd failed to break a single fiber of those planks. Staring at my right foot like it was a dead rat on the end of my shaking leg, I dragged my sorry ass out of the training hall.

I was out, and I'd not even passed stage one.

Ashamed, I was seriously considering not even attending the nationals to support my team members who *did* break their planks.

And worse—my faith in creative visualization was gone. It had failed me in my most desired goal. But this wasn't the end of the story. I was about to discover the first lesson of creative visualization.

Lesson 1: Be Unattached to the "How"— Instead Focus on the "What" and the "Why"

I'd presumed that what would get me to my goal of winning the championship was the "how"—me breaking that wood in the first trial, which would lead to the next, and so on. But I'd failed.

Little did I know that I was about to learn that as long as you focus on the "what" (getting to the US Open) and the "why" (because it was my passion), the "how" will take care of itself. And the "how" turned out to be a stroke of luck nobody could have called.

After spending the saddest week of my seventeen-year-old life so far sulking, I finally got to the point where I accepted my fate. And the time had come to be a good teammate. I ended up sitting alone in the stadium to watch the best players in Malaysia fight it out for that spot at the US Open. And thank God I did.

There I was, sitting with my hood up on the sidelines, supporting Daniel, one of my teammates at the time. He'd just fought an incredible match, surely landing him a spot in the US Open. He was a similar height and build to me, and he'd made it. But to my surprise, he came limping toward me at the end of the match.

"Vishen, I think I injured my foot."

Wow, really?

"My next competition is the wood-breaking round. But I feel like I might have a hairline fracture. If I break the wood I'll screw up my foot even more than it already is."

I nodded in silence.

"Would you take my spot?"

Wait, what?

"It's just for the wood breaking, Vishen. Do you have your Taekwondo uniform?"

Funnily enough, I did. I'd shoved it in my backpack that morning, as I always did. I'd watched way too many Superman cartoons and figured that I too could save lives or catch a bad guy in my crisp, white Taekwondo robe one day. I'd always had this fantasy of walking down the street, only to witness a poor old lady get her purse stolen by a robber. Upon witnessing this atrocity I'd dive into a nearby phone booth, do a lightning-fast change, and pop out again fully dressed for the occasion, ready to kick the robber's ass and save grandma's purse. True story.

So anyway, I'd come prepared.

Before I knew it, I was there dressed in full gear representing my class in the Malaysian Taekwondo championship, even though I was never meant to be at that competition in the first place. And once again, I was facing three planks of wood.

In my mind's eye, they mocked me. "Hahahahaha!" they laughed with their annoying wooden faces. "You think you can break us, do you?"

But I was audaciously optimistic. The universe had somehow delivered me a second chance.

The whistle blew. Deep breath, high-pitched *heia!*

KICK.

KICK.

KICK.

This time, I heard the applause.

I turned to look at my handiwork.

Plank one: broken.

Plank two: broken.

Plank three: intact.

A second later, I heard a slow creak. Plank three: broken!

I smashed the fastest breaking time in the entire event at 52 seconds. And much to my delight, alongside Daniel, I won the gold medal.

We were both headed to the US Open 1993 Taekwondo Championship.

According to the creative visualization advocates, the practice can often bring about synchronicities and unexpected "coincidences" that allow your desires to manifest despite the odds. So even though I failed the first time, I got exactly what I'd visualized in the end. I broke the wood, and I was going to the US Open. I just didn't get the victory I wanted in the exact way I expected. The "how" took care of itself in the end.

A whole new path to my "what"—getting to the US Open—had opened for me.

So I had a eureka moment: there was no need to obsess over *how* I'd smash my goals.

I showed up at the US Open, ready for the moment of truth.

And here I would learn the second lesson of creative visualization.

Lesson 2: Be Really Clear on What You Want

At the US Open in Colorado Springs, it was now time for me to actually go up against another human as opposed to a defenseless plank of wood in a sparring competition. This was it. My dream was coming true!

I approached the ring confidently. But when I clocked eyes on my opponent, my heart dropped into my training shoes.

I was up against Glenn Rybak—the Dutch national champion.

Fan-f*cking-tastic, I thought to myself sarcastically.

If you know anything about Dutch people, you know that these are some of the tallest people in the world. And if you know anything about Taekwondo, you know that more than anything, it's a kicking art form. So when you have the legs of a sexy giraffe, you have an inherent advantage.

So there I was, face-to-face, or should I say face to chest, with Glenn Rybak. And just as I was about to give him my best shot, adrenaline coursing through my veins, I heard the whistle blow.

"Kid, you can't go in there with glasses!" the ref shouted as he ushered me out of the ring.

I forgot to mention that back then, I wore specs. And trust me, I didn't wear them for style. I *needed* them. I was myopic with a minus seven hundred prescription. If he took them from me, I was screwed.

"I understand, ref, but these are sports glasses . . . these ones don't break . . ." I begged.

"No, kid. That might be okay in Malaysia, but not in this country. In America, everybody sues everybody for everything. Those things break and blind you, you could sue us for millions of dollars. We can't take that risk."

My face was blank.

I was a dead guy walking.

But I did as I was told.

I stepped into the ring once more, semiblind, and I heard the whistle blow. I puffed up my chest and Giraffe Man's silhouette began to move in front of me. At least, I *thought* he was in front of me: he could have been to my left, or my right, or hovering in midair for all I knew. I couldn't see a thing. Just a few seconds in, as I was trying my best to figure out where the hell his limbs were . . . BANG. I fell to the floor.

Part human, part giant, this guy's leg reach (and strength) was tremendous.

I managed to stagger to my feet. I wasn't done yet and if I could just see—BANG.

Before I could even finish my courageous thought, I became the official Fastest Knockout in the 1993 US Open Taekwondo Championship. Thirty-six seconds.

I was carried out on a stretcher.

When I woke up in the hospital, I had some time to reflect on what the hell had happened.

What went wrong?

If, by the laws of attraction and creative visualization "what you see is what you get," why did this happen?

That's simple. It happened that way because that's what I set myself up for.

I got *exactly* what I'd visualized.

When I was at home preparing for my time in the States, I saw myself breaking the wood. I saw myself putting on my robe with the word "MALAYSIA" sewn on the back. I saw myself step into the ring with confidence. I saw those bright lights on me. I got all that.

I only wish I'd seen myself actually *walk* out of the US Open, as opposed to being carried out on a stretcher!

So this was the second lesson of creative visualization. Be very, very specific in what you visualize.

Don't learn this lesson the hard way, like I did. You must see your accomplished goal through to the very end, declaring "May this or something even better manifest."

Because yes, I'd seen myself enter the ring, but I'd never given a second thought as to how I'd perform in it, how I'd feel in it, or how I'd leave it.

I was so taken aback by the idea of actually making it to the US Open that I hadn't bothered to contemplate what I actually wanted out of the experience.

Be Careful What You Wish For: Research Suggests You'll Get It

Has anybody ever told you to *be careful what you wish for*? Or perhaps they've warned you against being pessimistic because you'll create a "self-fulfilling prophecy"?

Well, there's actually some truth in that. Because this stuff works both ways. If you continuously think about something and convince yourself it's going to happen, for better or worse, it usually ends up happening.

And there's research to prove it.

What science is beginning to see is that creative visualization is one of the best-kept secrets of all time when it comes to shaping the world around you.

Athletes have been using this for decades, before it was cool. They knew that what the brain visualizes, the body responds to. In a study conducted on basketball players, Dr. Biasiotto of the University of Chicago proved the power of creative visualization. He tested two groups of players—one group who trained by actually shooting physical hoops and another who merely visualized the same training. He found that the percentage of improvement between both groups varied by just 1 percent!

Yep, players who solely *visualized* themselves training were pretty much as effective at scoring as the players who practiced in real life.

Visualizing yourself performing, in more ways than one, is almost as much of a bulletproof preparation as doing the real thing. Weird, right?

It gets weirder. A study known as the finger abduction experiment showed that if you take two groups of people, one of them exercising their fingers in a grabbing motion, and the other simply visualizing the same motion, both groups get the same increase in muscular strength.

Think about that for a second.

Seeing yourself exercising from the comfort of your couch has a very similar effect on your muscles as actually hitting the gym.

Mind *blown*, right?

That's creative visualization for you.

You can also heal yourself via the mind too. Heard of imagery therapy? José Silva, the guy who wrote *The Silva Method* (the same book that inspired me to use creative visualization to get to the US Open), tested this theory and proved that this process accelerates the body's natural healing mechanisms.

Dr. O. Carl Simonton, a world-renowned specialist in radiology and oncology, stated that "the Silva system, I would say, is the most powerful single tool that I have to offer patients."

This was the same incredible doctor who taught the imagery technique to 159 patients with "incurable" cancer. They'd been given twelve months to live. But after using creative visualization, out of all the participants:

- 63 were alive and well
- 14 showed no signs of cancer
- 12 had cancer regression/reductions in tumors
- 17 were stable

And the average expected survival rate had doubled to 24.4 months. Furthermore, all of these gobsmacking results manifested just *four* months after the experiment had begun.

Luckily, I haven't been faced with the task of healing my own cancer. But what I did do was heal my skin with creative visualization.

When I was a teenager, I had a major problem with my skin. I had more pimples than I could count, and it was seriously affecting my confidence. For five years various dermatologists had tried to help with all kinds of weird solutions, but none prevailed.

So I set about using creative visualization, the process I learned in José Silva's book, to heal it. And I did. In five weeks.

Five years of suffering had ended in five weeks due to the mere thoughts of clear skin. It goes without saying that that settled it. I was a self-proclaimed miracle and would forever be a die-hard Silva Method fan.

I actually have my own Silva Method course on Mindvalley; it's called the Silva Ultramind System. It's the newest version of the protocol, based on José's final discoveries before he passed in 1999. José's family asked me to be the face of this updated program so as to spread it to as many people as possible. The Silva Method is now officially part of Mindvalley and one of our most popular programs.

Apart from the miraculous and pretty immediate results it can cause in your own life (you'll have to see those for yourself), creative visualization has also been proven to:

1. Activate your creative subconscious, which will begin to generate new plans to help you hit your goals.
2. Reprogram your brain to be sharper and more sensitive to any signs or resources that will allow you to achieve your dreams faster (more on that in the next chapter; it's called your reticular activating system).
3. Build up your internal motivation levels so you can take active steps toward the future you desire.
4. Strengthen your brain's neuroplasticity (aka your ability to create neural pathways) around the achievement of your dream goals.

So, ready to give it a go?

The Three-Year Rule: Building Your Personal Vision

In the envisioning your future section of the 6 Phase Meditation, you'll be homing in on what you want to manifest in three years' time. That's *three* years. This time frame is very deliberate, because as humans we often overestimate what we can achieve in a year, and seriously underestimate what we can achieve in three years.

But a hell of a lot can happen in three years.

You could have completed a full mathematics degree at the world's best university.

You could have met the man or woman of your dreams and tied the knot.

You could even have packed in your job and founded your own company in three years. People do it all the time.

Have you ever heard the phrase "once in a blue moon"? People use it to refer to something that happens rarely. That's because blue moons happen only once every *three* years!

Three, you could say, is a magic number.

Anyway, bottom line is, three years may not seem too far ahead, but miraculous things can happen within that time frame.

So Phase 4 is all about visualizing your life within that time frame. This is your kid-in-a-candy-store moment, so take your pick.

Do you desire a body that's healthy, fit, and strong?

Do you want a passionate love relationship?

Do you want kids?

Maybe you'd prefer to focus on the success of your business or career.

Alternatively, you might want to visualize some incredible experiences, like traveling the world, forging new connections, and finding inner peace. Go wild, because the choice is yours.

There are no rules here except this one. You must, must, must choose something that *you* want.

Please note the italicized *you*.

We're not setting ourselves up to accomplish someone else's dreams, nor are we merely regurgitating what our parents and teachers told us we *should* want. The classic, successful linear lifestyle isn't everyone's dream.

Oftentimes what we *think* we want and what we *actually* want are two very different things. That's more often than not due to these overbearing societal influences.

So how do we know which desires are birthed from our souls and which ones are pure conditioning?

When you're trying to figure out if something is right for you, be it a new job or a new partner, take out a pen and paper and write down what you really want to see in your life. Be specific, be clear. Write down what you want for every category in your life.

The best method to do this is by writing a life manifesto.

So before you dive into visualizing some glorious aspect of your life three years out, set aside some time to do the exercise below.

The Life Manifesto Technique by Jon and Missy Butcher

Jon and Missy Butcher are two incredible entrepreneurs and all-around beautiful people. It was this power couple who created the globally celebrated Lifebook approach for goal setting.

I'm a big Lifebook fan and after doing the program in 2010, I decided to bring Lifebook to Mindvalley. Jon, Missy, and I are now business partners, and Lifebook is the primary goal-setting method used across the Mindvalley platform. The manifesto technique you're seeing here is part of this detailed Lifebook approach. I've simplified and shared it here to help you get really clear on your personal vision.

When you create your Lifebook, you uncover all your dreams that directly link to every single aspect of the human experience, with absolutely nothing left to chance. Lifebook itself is an eighteen-hour program that results in your creating a hundred-plus-page book with a vision and plan for your most glorious life. We won't have time to cover the whole curriculum here, but I'll share the basics of the "manifesto technique" from Lifebook to help you perfect Phase 4.

According to Jon and Missy, an incredible way to identify and manifest your life vision is by putting pen to paper and writing out what a day in your dream life would be like in an official manifesto.

That's it. Just one day.

But first, in order to make your vision as authentic and true to you as possible, you have to get clear on what you want from the twelve Lifebook categories:

Health and fitness

Intellectual life

Emotional life

Character

Spiritual life

Love relationship

Parenting

Social life

Financial

Career

Quality of life

Life vision

(That last category is basically the accumulation of the preceding eleven categories; it's what your life would look like if you had all the other categories exactly as you'd want them to be—aka your manifesto.)

It's worth noting that the Lifebook process is incredibly thorough, and when done correctly, you'll be spending several hours on each category over six weeks. You'll deep-dive into what's most important to you and why. You'll make plans and take inspired action to make it all happen. But by the end of the activities, you'll know exactly what goals you're aiming for in every single aspect of your human existence.

So, again, if you're serious about this, the very best thing you can do for yourself is the Lifebook online program. You can find it on www.mindvalley.com/lifebook.

Once you're crystal clear on all twelve of your Lifebook categories, you're ready to begin writing your Life Vision Manifesto based on your ideal day. But you'll do it in the *present tense*—as if you're living your dream life right now.

For inspiration, Jon gave me permission to share his own manifesto with you in this book.

Jon affirms that "this is the controlling document of our lives. It guides every decision we make—and it is the primary tool Lifebookers use to *truly* achieve the life of their dreams."

JON'S LIFE VISION MANIFESTO
CREATION DATE: JANUARY 2017

DUE DATE: JANUARY 2022

Missy and I have achieved simplicity on the far side of complexity and created our own version of heaven, right here on earth.

We live a life of luxury, adventure, and passion. We have the freedom to do what we want, when we want, where we want, with whom we want. We have an extraordinary life that works at a high level in every important area. And the hours of our days are OURS.

FREEDOM is our core value. We wake up every day in our beautiful home in Hawaii and ask ourselves, "What do we want this day to be about? The biggest project we've ever worked on? Nothing? Painting? Traveling?"

Life is a PLAYGROUND—a canvas for us to paint. We live in our unique ability. Our work consists entirely of creative projects that we are uniquely qualified to do. We don't spend time doing anything we don't truly want to do. This means we CREATE: write, record, design, produce, and BUILD.

We have a higher quality of life than ever before, which is really saying a lot! And yet, it costs almost NO MONEY to maintain (that being said, we have LOTS of money)! Our lifestyle is autonomous, self-sustaining, and self-sufficient. We have a beautiful food forest, a natural meat locker, and an ocean that provides most of our food. We're off the grid, out of the matrix, and completely nondependent on the government.

I work on business two mornings a week—and the rest of my time is my own to spend with Missy and the kids, studying, exercising, working on creative projects, planning the next day's activities, or whatever the fuck else I want to do. We spend plenty of time in nature . . . and we'll make our environment in Hawaii more and more beautiful over the years. Our "temple-home" will be my life's masterpiece, so that project is how I'll spend most of my time in 2022 and beyond.

In 2022, there's a relaxed and effortless flow to our days. They are rewarding and full. We take a walk together every evening. We watch every sunset together every night. In the evenings, we are FILLED from the day rather than drained by it. We bring positive, loving energy to the dinner table. We talk about meaningful things.

We laugh A LOT. We are relaxed, healthy, happy, and fulfilled.

Our Hawaii nights are simply MAGICAL. Missy and I have deep intimacy and an absolutely amazing sex life (indescribable, actually). It's healing, exciting, adventurous, and SO

MUCH FUN. We're in extraordinary physical shape for our age—or ANY age, for that matter! We are twin flames and soul mates in every way.

In 2022, we'll spend a lot of time helping our kids define their goals and achieve their dreams. Our kids and grandkids are healthy, happy, and SO ALIVE. They are BRIGHT LIGHTS—nothing has dampened them, because we dropped out of the rat race/matrix just before the dampening process began.

Missy and I have a rich social life in Hawaii. We don't spend time with ANYONE we don't love, admire, and respect. We hang out with fantastic people who enrich our lives and enhance our fun. Our best friends are always happy to travel to paradise to see us. We invest a lot in our friends. We travel with and enjoy them.

We're doing our "soul-work," helping others in all that we do, and earning a profit proportionate to the value we create. We help singles, couples, and families live better lives and achieve their dreams.

ALL our companies are AUTOMATED and doing better than we ever imagined. Lifebook is the world's premier personal development company—transforming lives on a massive scale. Purity is one of America's fastest-growing businesses—transforming a $100 billion industry. Precious Moments provides joy, comfort, and hope to millions around the world. Black Star is helping people heal from addiction. Our entire family is crushing Lifebook for Families. And Jon-AndMissy.com is where our life work comes together philosophically. It's the most amazing portfolio of companies that a couple could ever own—and we couldn't be more proud of what we've created!

Missy and I have a very high net worth and no debt. Despite our wealth, our financial life is simple, understandable, organized, and optimized. No complicated schemes, no fussy investments. We've cut expenses to create the biggest gap EVER between our income and fixed expenses, so we are FINANCIALLY FREE! Cash is more abundant than ever, we are surrounded by wealth—and we are living really, really WELL.

We live in PARADISE. Truly. We have created our own personal vision of heaven on earth. We are fully centered. We are happy. We are creative. We are fulfilled. We are ultra-healthy. We are energized. We have an extraordinary love life. We have our ideal career. We have financial abundance. We have an extraordinary relationship with every one of our kids. We enjoy truly amazing friendships. We RELAX a lot and enjoy our life, without feeling at all guilty about the immense amount of leisure time we have . . .

And that makes perfect sense, because our LIFE is our work.

Jon told me that he wrote that beautiful manifesto five years ago. And guess what?

Jon and Missy are living every single word of that life *right now*.

If that's not inspiring, I don't know what is.

Now, when you attempt to write a manifesto like this, it is quite likely that you'll end up focusing on what you're currently putting your energy into and ignoring what might be even more important. That's because what you need isn't on your radar yet.

For example, you might see yourself bossing your career, but neglect to see yourself healthy.

You might see yourself with a six-figure bank balance, but forget to see yourself in a happy relationship.

On the other hand, you might see yourself falling madly in love, but forget to dedicate some brainpower to your finances.

You want to aim for it all. And to help you spot any gaps in your vision, Jon and I created a simple twenty-minute assessment you can take right now. After answering all the questions, it'll produce a report to let you know where you're acing life (and what you're neglecting) in the twelve categories we shared earlier.

You can take the assessment anytime at life.mindvalley.com. It's free.

Thus, in summary, to get clear on your life vision for Phase 4:

1. Take the assessment at life.mindvalley.com.
2. Take some time and write your life manifesto.
3. Use what you've written in your manifesto to guide your daily visualization in Phase 4.

Here's how Phase 4 will play out in the 6 Phase Meditation.

The Envisioning Your Future Protocol

Step 1—Choose Your Goals for the Future

I'm going to assume that by now you have written out the goals that you want to achieve in your manifesto (or at least thought about them).

These goals might include:

- Traveling the world
- Finding the love of your life
- Buying your dream house
- Becoming fluent in a foreign language
- Building your own business
- Achieving financial independence
- Having children/adopting
- Skydiving/hiking/racing for charity
- Healing from illness
- Becoming a teacher, coach, or mentor

You want to choose the goals you wish to achieve *three* years from now, remember? Be audacious and unapologetic about what you want, just like Jon and Missy.

Step 2—Pull Up Your Mental Screen

As you begin to meditate on Phase 4, you'll imagine that there's a giant TV screen in your mind's eye, and you're watching everything play out like a movie.

You'll imagine that the screen is six feet in front of you, fifteen degrees above the line of the horizon. This is what José Silva's research found provided the best results.

I know that's pretty specific, but there's a good reason we use this technique. You see, it's been proven that if you're actively looking beyond your eyelids with your pupils pointing slightly upward, your brain begins to produce alpha waves. And altered states of consciousness are exactly what we want to access to max out the effects of creative visualization.

So switch off your electrical devices. Eyes forward and up, everyone. The movie is about to begin. (And it's going to be the best damn movie you've ever seen.)

You're going to see those palm trees blowing in the breeze as well as those droplets of water on the outside of your piña colada glass on the beach in Hawaii.

You're going to see that delectably cute puppy you've always wanted licking your nose like you were watching a cuter version of *Marley and Me*.

You get the picture (literally). Whatever it is you're choosing to see, even though it's a goal for three years ahead, you're going to feel all the emotions that you would experience as if this movie were real and happening right now. That brings us to step 3.

Step 3—Feel It All with Your Five Senses

The more senses you use, the better.

Now it's time to lose yourself in creative visualization. See, hear, taste, smell, and feel your dreams play out to perfection.

When you use all your senses in creative visualization, it creates a feeling. It creates emotions of joy, gratitude, excitement, peace, comfort, and enthusiasm. And according to José Silva, if you capture the emotions, you're onto a winner. When you experience the emotions that you'll be feeling once these dreams come true, you're priming both your brain and the universe to give you exactly what you want.

For extra manifestation points, don't forget to explore how hitting your goals would positively impact others too.

This is daydreaming at its best (and most enjoyable). So breathe deep and revel in the pleasure of experiencing your goals manifesting in advance.

Now it's your turn to kick ass with the powerful effects of creative visualization.

I can honestly credit creative visualizations for all my major successes in life. It led me to exactly where I'm at today. I visualized my move to the United States to follow my dreams. My company, Mindvalley, hitting $100 million in revenue was visualized too. I visualized my two beautiful children, whom I adore, in my mind before they were born. This stuff works.

So go wild . . .

Don't underestimate what you're capable of achieving.

Screw realism.

Most people are realists, and that's understandable. *Realist* sounds like *real*, and everyone wants to "be real." It's the cool thing to be, and

I've got no doubt that realists think that's the smartest way to go about their lives.

But it's a giant, self-sabotaging trap, because in being "realistic," people assess their realities as they are now and base their futures on it. It's the "it's happened before so it will happen again" mentality, which is extremely limiting.

There was a time not so long ago when women didn't have the right to vote. Do you believe for a second that the suffragettes would have gotten anywhere if not for their *un*realisticness?

For progress of any kind to happen, what we need are visionaries, not realists.

So I'd encourage you to dream as big as you dare. It's like Richard Branson once said:

If your dreams don't scare you, they are too small.

Before you proceed to the next chapter, open up your Mindvalley app and launch the 6 Phase Meditation program. From there, you can jump into the full interactive lesson for Phase 4: A Vision for Your Future. The lesson is just a few minutes long and will recap some of the most important points in this chapter. Upon completion, you can then dive straight into the meditation audio where I'll guide you through the envisioning protocol. It will take less than five minutes but will help lock in the fourth phase of your practice.

CHAPTER 5

PHASE 5

Mastering Your Day

Carpe diem quam minimum credula postero.

HORACE

Translated from Latin as the undeniably overused phrase "seize the day," the short and snappy *carpe diem* exclamation has some pretty intriguing origins.

History claims that it was Quintus Horatius Flaccus (what a name, right?) who uttered this phrase way back in 23 BCE. He's known in the English-speaking world as the oversimplified "Horace," which I find really funny.

But this whole idea of living for today and making an effort to squeeze as much juice out of life as possible is a lot older than Horace. The sentiment has run through the lines of ancient Greek literature, poetry, philosophical lectures, and prayers for millennia.

And whether you studied history or not, you have undoubtedly been told in one way or another by your loved ones, teachers, employers, and preachers to treat this day as if it were your last. In one way or another, you've been instructed to do exactly what Horace taught his compatriots thousands of years ago while sporting his fetching Roman toga and sandals.

Your Future, Today

So why do so many of us neglect and deny the magic that is today?

Dragging themselves out of bed in the morning with no appropriate action plan whatsoever, a lot of people don't realize that today *is* the future. And the importance of setting an intention for it is just as important as setting your goals for the long term.

It's just as vital to plan for today as it is to dream of your life in three years' time, as we did in Phase 4: A Vision for Your Future. It's thanks to the actions you take today that your dreams will manifest.

Just like you did in Phase 4, you're going to pull up that giant TV screen and see your awesome future play out in front of you. Only this time it's not the future that awaits in three years' time. It's all about the next twenty-four hours.

Another difference from the previous phase: you'll split your day into sections that are meaningful to you. So you'll see the upcoming twenty-four hours as having several segments, like a juicy futuristic orange.

The Power of "Segment Intending"

Philosopher Esther Hicks best explains the concept known as "segment intending," and Phase 5 is based on this protocol.

If you're not familiar with Esther's work, just know that she's no ordinary woman. Her ability to channel Source, aka "Abraham," has allowed her to download deep, divine insights many of us don't have the pleasure (yet) of accessing. It was, in fact, her work that inspired the 2006 documentary *The Secret*, which went on to sell five hundred thousand copies, making it the best-selling DVD in history.

One of the divine insights Esther famously channeled was the idea that you can, and *should*, pre-envision and visualize your upcoming day as a series of "segments" that are meaningful to you.

Here's how a typical day might flow in segments:

07:00–08:30: Waking up, meditating, preparing breakfast, and
    getting ready for work
08:30–09:00: Commuting to work
09:00–13:00: Morning meetings/work
13:00–14:00: Lunch break with colleagues
14:00–17:00: Work
17:00–17:30: Commute home
17:30–19:00: Prepare and eat dinner
19:00–21:00: Kick back and watch Netflix with partner
21:00–22:00: Enjoy incredible sex with said partner
22:00–07:00: Sleep

And you might top off your segments by declaring a positive affirmation after you run through each of them with all your senses:

"My morning will be filled with energy and joy."

"My workday will be highly productive, sociable, and fun."

"My lunch will be delicious, with a beautiful backdrop of music and laughter."

"My commute home will be pleasant and free from traffic."

"I will find something amazing and moving to watch on Netflix."

"Sex with my partner will be passionate and oxytocin-filled."

I'm sure you get the picture.

Although our segments will vary (maybe you're not working, but rather studying, traveling, or taking some time out right now), no matter what, the segment intending exercise remains the same; you're going to see each and every segment unfolding beautifully.

From Esther's standpoint, winging it through our days isn't an optimal way to live out twenty-four hours of pure possibility. Rather, we want to become "well-disciplined people."

In her words, "Well-disciplined people decide how they want their day to unfold."

And the most optimal way to communicate (to the divine) how you want your day to unfold is via segment intending.

For the Skeptics and Optimists

If you're new to this whole concept and are a little skeptical, Esther advises that you start by saying, "Wouldn't it be nice if . . ." followed by your intention. That way, you're still engaging in the segment manifestation process while honoring your healthy doubt. For example, "Wouldn't it be nice if my boss appreciated me in our meeting today."

On the other hand, if you're already a big believer in the power of your own mind, go for a command. For example, "Today, my favorite song, 'Bohemian Rhapsody,' is going to play on the radio when I'm driving to work."

Just play the game and see what happens.

I say, if you've got the confidence, use it. Your unshakable faith makes for an incredibly potent catalyst when it comes to daily manifestation. It's like Jim Carrey said: "Hope is a beggar. Hope walks through the fire. Faith leaps over it."

So come on, guys. Let's be like Jim.

The Science Behind Why All This Works

Of course, all this begs the question . . . will this daily intention-setting embedded in the 6 Phase Meditation, which asks only two minutes of your day, actually work?

In short, the answer is a resounding and unshakable *yes*.

Yes, this *does* work. And it does so thanks to one of your brain's lesser-known magic tricks: the reticular activating system. I'll refer to your reticular activating system from now on as the RAS.

In a nutshell, your RAS comprises a truckload of nerves that sit in

145

your brain stem, just waiting to filter out any unuseful information from your surroundings. And thank goodness it does, because now more than ever we're surrounded by the incessant, bright, flashy stimuli of the twenty-first century. It's thanks to your RAS that all the important stuff—the voice of your loved one in a crowd, your job responsibilities, fire hazards, and threats, for example—get prioritized in your attention at the appropriate time.

So you could say, then, that the RAS takes whatever you want to focus on and creates a specific filter for it. It then sifts through all the incoming data during the day and presents only the pieces of information that are important to you. Furthermore, this takes absolutely no effort on your part, as it's all automatic. Amazing, right?

So when the biblical Saint Matthew warned us, "Seek, and ye shall find," he wasn't lying. What you focus on every day will come to you, and thanks to your RAS filter, your brain will stop at nothing to seek it out.

In most psychology papers that talk about the RAS, the example they tend to give is the one about white Volkswagens.

If you own a white Volkswagen and you're driving it down the highway, you're much more likely to notice other white Volkswagens cruising down the highway too. That's because your brain is aware that you yourself are driving one. The same theory applies when you make a declaration about your day.

If you decide that you're going to have an amazing lunch break filled with great food, even better company, and a beautiful ambience, you are commanding your brain to notice these things, in advance. And if you do happen to go to a restaurant and the waiter messes up your order—say, they dared to serve you non-gluten-free bread—

you're more likely to ignore these imperfections. Your brain will be way too busy noticing the incredible taste of your guac and Monterey Jack cheese combo, the pretty candles, and the sparkling conversation.

Overall, when that lunch ends, despite being served the wrong food, you're way more likely to perceive it as a great, highly successful lunch break, because that's what you programmed your brain to do. Period.

Does this make you a bit delusional?

Yes.

But it also makes you a happier person and puts you in an infinitely better mood on a day-to-day basis. I'm all for that kind of delusional behavior. I'd rather be joyfully deluded than bitchy, negative, and whiny over tiny things that bother negative people every day.

The Spiritual Standpoint

Now that you've enjoyed the unadulterated science, here's the spiritual standpoint.

When we set an intention for how we want something to unfold, many spiritual teachers believe that it's more likely to manifest organically. It's called deliberate creation and works according to the Law of Attraction, which we briefly touched on in the previous chapter.

This theory has less hard science to back it up, but those who advocate this concept say that when we make a decision, it becomes a cosmic choice that directly moves us into that potential future.

Esther takes this idea further, and makes it all the more beautiful, claiming that when we connect to the magic of manifestation, we become creative gods enjoying the experience of being human.

147

The Added Feel-Good Bonuses of Phase 5

When you decide to have a great day, it has a big ripple effect. Great days end up evolving into great weeks. Great weeks then evolve into great months, and great months to great years. And great years evolve into an absolutely epic life.

It all starts with making a firm decision in two minutes during the 6 Phase Meditation on how you're going to seize the day.

As well as setting yourself up for an awesome day (and life) filled with more optimism and joy, Phase 5 also feels incredibly pleasurable in real time.

Just like Phase 4: A Vision for Your Future, Phase 5 is another kid-in-a-candy-store opportunity. Remember the best part—your brain has no idea that these incredible things aren't *actually* happening as you meditate. When you see a happy, flowing day in your mind's eye, you'll feel all the positive emotions that you'd feel if they were happening for real. Your emotional and physical body will react on a biochemical level.

Although it's all just in your head (for now), the dopamine, serotonin, oxytocin, and endorphins are real.

And when you're all Nina Simone *feeling good* as you go about your day, other people will benefit too. Because every single person you come into contact with will share your positive vibes. Happiness is infectious. And that's an infection humanity could do with right now.

Here's the protocol.

The Mastering Your Day Protocol

Step 1—Pull Up Your Mental Screen

Imagine that huge TV screen right in front of you, where you can watch your day play out.

Remember what I told you about the segments? You'll start from the beginning and proceed in chronological order. If you're stuck on where to start, it's worth remembering what you chose to focus on previously for your three-year goal in Phase 4. Then you can integrate a small step toward it into your daily routine.

Say in Phase 4 you imagined becoming a world-renowned author. In this phase, you might see yourself spending an hour of your upcoming day in your favorite café, working on your book ideas, as one of your segments.

If you envisioned a fit, healthy body, see yourself taking a step toward that goal at some point in your day. Maybe you'll see yourself making a green smoothie or going for a long walk on your lunch break; whatever fits.

If you aren't practicing first thing in the morning (which is recommended), don't worry; just start imagining what's going to happen after you open your eyes from the meditation.

Step 2—See and Feel Your Entire Day Going Amazingly

Now you'll see the chronological movie of your day from morning till night.

Just like you did in the previous phase, you'll see, hear, taste, smell, and feel your upcoming day play out to perfection. At the

149

beginning of every segment, don't forget to set a verbal intention, such as "My breakfast will be nutritious and fill me with energy," all the way to "My sleep will be deep and restorative."

This is your time of dedicated daydreaming for your day. Don't be afraid to be optimistic, even if it feels like having a great day is an impossible feat due to the challenges that may await you. Be brave and have faith that the highest and best is going to manifest and that you'll be that healing presence on whichever room you enter.

If nothing else, have faith in the science and your brain's reticular activating system. This is anything but a waste of time.

So there you have it. You've completed Phase 5. I love this phase because it's bringing you from meditation to action. After all, the 6 Phase Meditation is not meant to be one of those meditations where, when you come out, you feel all floaty and ready for a nap. It's meant to be a meditation that relaxes you but gets you ready to conquer the world.

There's a big difference.

Who knew that you could simply *decide* to have a kick-ass day? Don't you wish they had taught us this stuff at school? When I learned that I could choose how my days would unfold as well as (most of) the events that came to be, I became an infinitely happier man. It empowered me.

Sure, nobody has ever asked that pigeon to poop on their windshield, but what they *can* choose is where their brain laser-focuses its attention. What they can choose is to train their optimism, positivity, and mind-set for the day ahead.

Can you imagine what would happen if each and every person woke up in the morning with the intention to have a beautiful day? To make themselves and others happy? To eat well, be mindful, and enjoy the seemingly mundane? To invest, even if it's just a little, in their long-term goals with a tiny step per day?

As Mother Teresa said:

Yesterday is gone. Tomorrow has not yet come. We have only today. Let us begin.

So what are you waiting for?
Go ahead and *carpe* this *diem*!

Before you proceed to the next chapter, open up your Mindvalley app and launch the 6 Phase Meditation program. From there, you can jump into the full interactive lesson for Phase 5: Mastering Your Day. The lesson is just a few minutes long and will recap some of the most important points in this chapter. Upon completion, you can then dive straight into the meditation audio where I'll guide you through the perfect day protocol. It will take less than five minutes but will help lock in the fifth phase of your practice.

CHAPTER 6

PHASE 6

The Blessing

You can search the entire universe and
not find a single being more worthy of love than you.

GAUTAMA BUDDHA

When I designed the 6 Phase Meditation, I wanted to create something rooted in science.

Because now more than ever, what humanity needs is the compass of science to help us distinguish snake oil from real medicine.

Having said that, science cannot explain *everything*, can it?

You've come to the only phase of the 6 Phase Meditation that will be a little threadbare in terms of solid, black-and-white evidence. But I still want you to partake in this short exercise—that of receiving a blessing from a higher power to commemorate your meditation practice.

It just so happens that the very subjects that science can't (yet) explain are also crucial to fill our lives with meaning. And although there's no conclusive research to prove that there's a higher power, a loving presence that's watching over us, 84 percent of humanity nonetheless believes this is the case.

That's because, at times against logic, we somehow *feel* it, *sense* it, and *intuit* it.

I, for one, believe to my core that I'm connected to a higher energy. That's not to say that I'm religious. I absolutely don't believe in the idea of an old bearded man in the sky who's judging my every move. Rather, my personal spiritual practice is a mixture of many of the world's religions plus some modern conveniences. I really don't believe in having just one religion—that idea just seems unnatural to me when there's so much beauty and wisdom to be found in all of them. That said, none of the rituals, philosophies, and practices that resonate with me define my spirituality either.

So, although I definitely believe in a higher energy, my word for *It* is pretty interchangeable. God, Goddess, the Universe, the Great Spirit, my Spirit, Pachamama, Lord Shiva, Archangel Michael, the morphogenetic field, the Higher Self, Gaia, my Higher Self—you name it, I'll be fine with it.

Because really, in my eyes, we're all talking about the same thing.

And I believe that "thing," that energy, is something that we're plugged into at all times. I believe it's something that supports us, nurtures us, and has our back.

Like I said, although there's no solid proof, there are countless people who've claimed to have experienced the presence of God.

Some speak of angels, guides, and feelings of samadhi—in particular, those who've had near-death experiences.

So do we dismiss these people's stories because we haven't yet been able to replicate them in a lab?

Michael Beckwith on the Power of Asking for Divine Intervention

In November 2017, I listened to a story from Reverend Michael Beckwith that inspired me to think about life and the concept of "God" in a new way. Michael was onstage at A-Fest, in the middle of another one of his mind-blowing speeches when it happened, but to be honest, I wasn't really paying attention.

A-Fest was my festival, you see, and I was backstage syncing with the sound engineers, ensuring that everything in the auditorium was running like clockwork.

But there was this moment when, as I was speaking to the crew, I suddenly felt *very* compelled to pay attention to what Michael was saying and stopped midsentence. And at that particular moment in his talk, he was telling the audience about a time he'd nearly drowned just off the coast of Costa Rica.

Michael was swimming with his daughter when he was violently dragged away from shore by a totally unexpected riptide. Being an older man, he knew he didn't have the strength he had in his youth, and he quickly realized that he wasn't going to make it back to shore.

"Just keep swimming. Do not pay attention to the body. Just keep swimming," he repeated to himself over and over, attempting to calm himself as he got dunked under the colossal waves again, swallowing a cruel amount of seawater.

It was at that moment that Michael said the words:

Help me.

Now, Michael claims these words didn't come out of his mouth consciously. Moreover, there was nobody *physically* coming to help him. The only person around for miles was his daughter, who was now far away and safe on the beach.

After what felt like hours of underwater chaos, there was a quiet lull.

And from this divine silence, Michael shared that a small wave came up from behind him to give him a taste of forward momentum. Then another wave came, a little bigger this time. Then a third wave gave him some more momentum until finally, exhausted and injured, he managed to scramble his way onto the sand and into his daughter's arms.

Thank you, God. Thank you to whatever name you want to be called.

A few days later Michael began telling a friend of his, who also happens to be a medium, about his experience in Costa Rica. Before he could even get to the part where he got dragged under the riptide, his friend asked, "Can I look?" with a knowing glimmer in her eye.

After he gave her the go-ahead, the medium saw the scene in her mind's eye. "Wow! You, you asked for help out loud, right?" Michael nodded. She continued, "When you asked for help at that moment, an archangel swooped down and ruffled the water . . . three times for you to get out . . . ?"

That's exactly what happened, he whispered. Three waves pushed him to shore.

Michael shared with us that the whole experience had taught him a very powerful lesson: to have the humility to ask for help. And no help can be given from the ancestral, shamanic, divine, angelic (whatever you call it) realm to this physical dimension unless you do so clearly and directly.

Because while it's important to program your mind for success, just like you've done in the previous five phases of this book, it's also vital for us to be open to receiving help to make sure it happens.

Like Michael learned, there are always forces around us ready to help; we just have to ask. In his words, AQ (your *availability quotient* to that higher power) always trumps IQ (the mind's intellectual ability to manifest as a standalone force).

So that's what this final section of the 6 Phase Meditation is all about.

Expanding Your Availability Quotient

Although this phase is called "the blessing," it doesn't mean you're in for an enforced conversion. Nobody is going to flick holy water on your forehead against your will.

But the blessing does have its place here. As most people believe in a higher power, I thought it appropriate to honor that and make it an integral part of the 6 Phase Meditation.

Furthermore, it takes only a few seconds. You'll imagine a beautiful light coming down from the sky that represents your higher power. You'll then allow it to encapsulate your body before fully receiving the blessing (or in other words, the help you need).

In addition to honoring the spiritual beliefs of the meditator, I also included the blessing to bring a tangible close to the entire meditative practice so we set ourselves up for the day feeling complete and supported in our intentions.

But it was actually one of my most respected mentors, Srikumar Rao, who led to the final decision to include it.

Srikumar Rao is an internationally acclaimed business school professor, TED speaker, bestselling author, and founder of the Rao Institute. Commonly known as the "Buddha of business," Srikumar has taught at the London Business School, the Kellogg School of Management at Northwestern University, and the Haas School of Business at the University of California, Berkeley. And he has a way of combining spiritual wisdom with entrepreneurship in a way I've never seen before.

Having taught hundreds of MBA students to achieve success by refining their personal philosophies and "mental models," Srikumar is a major authority when it comes to living a fulfilling human existence.

When I was developing the 6 Phase Meditation, I listened to a talk Srikumar was doing on the psychology of success and happiness. He was preaching about how your mental models—that is, what you believe to be true about the world—will directly influence your experiences in it, be they positive or negative.

At the end of the talk, Srikumar was asked, repeatedly, to define which mental model was the very best to have. This is what he said:

The most important belief you can possess is the belief that the universe loves you. If you believe that the universe is always working in your favor, you will have a beautiful experience in this life.

The word *universe* is replaceable, by the way, with whichever word you deem most appropriate.

After hearing Srikumar say that this was the ultimate mental model out of the billions of other singular beliefs one could choose, I knew I had to conclude this special sequence with the blessing.

I'm of the opinion that, after meditating on Phase 6 and then going forth into your day believing you're not alone, believing you're loved and supported, you're in for an amazing time.

Not only that. Cumulatively, you're in for an amazing life of wonder and positivity.

The Blessing: Nobody Gets Left Behind

Now, if I may, I'd like to address those who choose not to believe in God (or any other word you might use to describe a higher power).

First, let me just say that I frickin' love atheists. They're some of the most interesting people I've ever met, with some of the sharpest minds out there, and being one doesn't exempt you from Phase 6. Not by a long shot.

I actually don't believe in a separate "God" either. I'm more of a pantheist, having a reverence for the entire universe—which Richard Dawkins, author of *The God Delusion*, describes as "sexed-up atheism."

So, atheist or religious, everyone can reap the same feelings of calm, collectedness, and support from Phase 6. Because even if you're a devout atheist, you can still connect to whatever power that you believe lies inside yourself.

Your inner power. Your resilience. Your inner reservoirs of strength. Your deep sense of knowing and wisdom. Your heart. Your brilliant mind.

Some people like to envision their older, wiser selves blessing them and supporting them. Go ahead and time travel twenty years ahead and draw inspiration from them.

Whatever you choose, you'll allow the best version of yourself to conclude your practice.

It's Your Turn to Receive Support

This part of the 6 Phase Meditation, as I said, is the shortest, easiest phase. But it can also be the most relaxing and pleasurable. It provides a refreshing contrast to the previous five phases.

If you think about it, up to now you've been pretty busy *giving*. You've been actively focusing on other people, sending your energy outward. You've meditated on compassion and gratitude. You've forgiven an asshole who hurt you. You poured your attention into what you want to manifest in three years' time, as well as how you want your day to unfold.

Phase 6 is your moment to be pleasantly passive, allowing someone/something else to envelop you in love and attention. And who better to do it than . . . the universe?

You'll connect with this abundant energy to not only bless your practice, integrating all of the previous five phases, but to make you feel supported as you take your first step into a brand-new day.

Because being human is pretty hard-core. Outside the comfortable confines of our bedroom walls where we start the day await potential challenges, roadblocks, and triggers. And no matter what your spiritual beliefs are, I feel we can all agree that we need support to navigate all of the good, the bad, and the ugly.

To prosper, unlock our inner genius, hit our goals, and jump into the unknown, we need all that energy. And the good news is that your higher power, or higher self, has it in bucketloads. It's infinite. The blessings will never run out. You just have to be open to receiving them.

The Blessing Protocol

Step 1—Call on Your Higher Power

Take a deep breath in and take a second to connect to your higher power, whatever that may be.

Try to feel the presence of your God/Goddess/spiritual force/higher self as opposed to thinking your way through the exercise and diving into a whole cognitive process about it. We're activating what Michael Beckwith described as your AQ (your availability quotient) here as opposed to your IQ.

Once you've forged a connection, it's time to invite in a blessing.

161

Step 2—Feel Your Higher Power as a Beam of Loving Light

Now imagine that blessing from your higher power as a beautiful golden or white light shining down from above. Feel the light. Sense the brightness and the comforting warmth of it, knowing it's filled with infinite power and energy.

Know that within this blessing is the official signal from the universe to go forth into your day and *carpe diem*. It's saying, "Yeah, all those intentions are fine by me, here's all the energy you'll need to make it happen." It's a confirmation that you're not alone. So let it in.

(If you're an atheist, this is the part where you call upon your inner power or an older, wiser version of yourself. Imagine you can feel their presence as this light too.)

Step 3—Allow the Light to Flow Through You

From there, imagine this light traveling its way through your head and going down your spine.

Then imagine the light expanding from your body to form a bubble around you. Imagine yourself enveloped in a shield of this loving, infinitely powerful light from your higher power, knowing that it's going to be with you for the rest of your day to protect you from negativity, support you, and fill you with all the qualities you need to flourish. This is your blessing.

Step 4—Thank Your Higher Power

Know that all your visions and intentions are now backed up by God/ the most badass version of yourself.

Take a second to enjoy that feeling and thank your (higher) power. You may bring the protocol to a close by using a mantra or prayer from your religion. Prayer hands, bow, cheeky smile, a whispered "thank you," whatever you choose.

Alternatively, you could close the protocol the way I do it and top it off with an imaginary fist pump to the universe. Then you're ready to gently bring yourself out of the meditation and get on with your amazing day.

Soak it all in and harness that blessing completely so you can go out there and kick butt with confidence.

Step 5—Close Your Meditation

Now you'll bring yourself out of the meditation after a count of five seconds.

If you are using the app to listen to the audio-guided meditation, I'll count you out gently, Silva Method–style. Here is the exact script I'll use:

> I will now count from one to five. When I reach the count of five, you will open your eyes, be wide awake, feeling fine and in perfect health.
> . . . One

... Two

... Three

Ready to open your eyes, feeling fine, and in perfect health.
... Four

... Five

Eyes open. Wide awake. Feeling fine and in perfect health. Feeling better than before.

And that's it. You're done. You've done everything you need to do to reach ultimate peace and happiness.

You've experienced connection with the world via compassion. You've enjoyed the feeling of fullness via gratitude. You've cleansed your soul of negative charges through forgiveness. You've set an amazing vision for your future—one you truly want. You've asked for a perfect day. And you've brought it all together with a blessing from that indescribable force that has traveled with you since the day you were born, and that will continue to be with you until the day you die.

Phase 6 takes only a few seconds, but it's worth its weight in gold, because any time we spend connected to something greater than ourselves is time well spent.

After all, we're so used to being the stars of our own show, we forget that we're not alone. No matter what you believe in, be it a god or a badass, an older and wiser version of yourself, you're supported.

And in order to succeed, to realize your true potential, you *need* that support.

So rely on a higher power.

Rely on that place deep within yourself that is infinitely powerful beyond measure.

Rely on one, the other, or both.

It doesn't matter.

Because one of the most ancient truths we'll ever learn is that *there's no difference between the two.*

Open up your Mindvalley app and launch the 6 Phase Meditation program. From there, you can jump into the full interactive lesson for Phase 6: The Blessing. The lesson is just a few minutes long and will recap some of the most important points in this chapter. Upon completion, you can then dive straight into the meditation audio where I'll guide you through the blessing protocol. It will take less than five minutes but will help lock in the sixth phase of your practice.

This is the final phase of the 6 Phase Meditation, so after you've consolidated your knowledge, you're ready to start meditating on the entire sequence. You'll find the full 6 Phase audio on the Mindvalley app (both on your 6 Phase mini-program and on the meditation tab).

CHAPTER 7

FROM PRACTICE TO MASTERY

The Final Word

A few years ago, I invited a brilliant man to give a talk at my office.

He went by the name of Tom Chi. You may well have heard of him. He's the cofounder of Google X and creator of the world's first prototype of the Google Glass augmented-reality device. This guy was an all-around genius, renowned for his ability to answer humanity's toughest questions in a way that combined cutting-edge science and deep, spiritual philosophy.

From the existence of God to virus evolution, Tom Chi and I would have many amazing discussions on stage together as well as on the Mindvalley podcast. I respect his work profusely.

On that particular day when Tom visited Mindvalley's office in Kuala Lumpur, he'd decided to give a talk on exponential technology and where the world was headed. My team was fascinated, and as the talk spilled over into a quick-fire Q&A, a brilliant employee of mine raised his hand and asked a question. It was this question, and its answer, that inspired my personal aspirations and goals in this lifetime.

"Tom, what's one thing you think we really need to be obsessed about to help make this world a better one?"

Tom paused for a few seconds. Then he responded:

"We need to create an exponential rise in human consciousness."

Tom went on to explain that the exponential technologies that are chartering the course of our future are becoming increasingly more powerful and dangerous. Nowadays, anyone can surf the dark web, buy themselves some C4 explosives, strap them to a $99 drone, and fly it into a building. And then with the push of a button, blow that building to smithereens with everyone in it.

The only thing preventing them from doing that? Their level of consciousness.

If we carry on this way, constantly scaling our technology while remaining stagnant in our consciousness evolution, a dark future awaits.

In other words, if we don't raise human consciousness, *we're done for.*

"Absolutely DONE for!" Tom emphasized.

Therefore, the biggest mission that we can ever embark on is the one that aims to level up human consciousness. To do so we need to understand that we're really in a great tug-of-war between two opposing evolutionary versions of the human mind.

The Primitive Mind vs. the Higher Mind

In his famous article "The Great Battle of Fire and Light," globally celebrated blogger (and one of my favorite philosophers) Tim Urban explains that being human is a constant battle between what he describes as the "Primitive Mind" and the "Higher Mind."

Far too often in the world today, we operate from the Primitive Mind.

The Primitive Mind could be seen as our ancestral animalistic software, which, contrary to what many choose not to believe, still resides as strongly as ever. It's the eat, procreate, repeat program. On the other hand, we have the Higher Mind—the highly advanced consciousness where all the ethical, wise, and spiritual magic happens.

The Chinese, and many others, would describe the Higher Mind as the heart and the Primitive Mind as the ego, but for the sake of this book, we'll follow Tim's definition.

The Primitive Mind experiences daily life in survival mode, in lack, and in competition. The Higher Mind lives life with presence, gratitude, and compassion.

The Primitive Mind believes struggle and competition are the keys to survival. The Higher Mind knows that we can tap into the power of positive thought and intention to manifest the future we desire.

The Primitive Mind is protective and loving only to those of the same family creed. The Higher Mind sees the illusions of borders, race, ethnicity, and culture and feels compassion toward all human beings, no matter how different they may appear.

The Primitive Mind drowns in negativity bias. The Higher Mind embraces all emotions and integrates them in a healthy way in the name of personal evolution.

The Primitive Mind is wild and untrainable. The Higher Mind is flexible, centered, and open.

The Primitive Mind feels alone in the world.

The Higher Mind sees the intricate connection between all life on Earth and understands that we are all part of something much bigger than ourselves.

The Higher Mind and the 6 Phase Meditation

So you see, the 6 Phase Meditation was designed specifically to move us toward the Higher Mind. Although we need some elements of it for our survival (such as our ability to fight or flee), ironically, the Primitive Mind that desperately attempts to keep us alive as individuals has the potential to end up destroying the human race.

So if we want to expand our level of consciousness to match the scarily high technological bar we've set, we need to activate the Higher Mind. Fast.

So that, reader, was the secret agenda behind teaching you the 6 Phase Meditation.

Because it turns out that all of the phases of this meditation—compassion, gratitude, forgiveness, humanity plus goal setting, and spirituality—don't just have the potential to save your skin as an individual. Meditating this way as a collective could end up saving us *all*.

Adding Our "Grain of Sand" to the Great Beach

Now that you're chewing on this newfound knowledge regarding the future of humanity, technology, and world-peace-inspiring higher consciousness, you might feel extra motivated to keep yourself on the straight and narrow with your meditation practice.

But I didn't set out to overwhelm you.

Fundamentally, you start off your meditation for *yourself*. And that's enough. It's more than enough.

You deserve love, peace, and happiness just as much as the next human, and this meditation will bring you that. You don't have to go violently protesting in the street against AI, whip plastic straws out of people's mouths, and walk barefoot around San Francisco in an attempt to show that you care about the Earth.

There's a beautiful, commonly used Spanish phrase that encompasses the value of small changes and how they end up being huge in the long term:

Hay que poner cada uno su granito de arena.
"Every individual must contribute their own grain of sand."

Meaning, if everyone throws in one tiny grain of sand, ultimately, that's how you get a beach worth visiting.

If every single individual meditated tomorrow morning, felt a sense of compassion and belonging, felt grateful and cleansed of resentment, and summoned the strength and inspiration to go out into the world and contribute, living every day as if it were their last . . .

171

. . . can you imagine what an amazing place this planet would be?

But before that happens, we're going to need some strong pioneers who perfect their inner worlds so they can make a difference in the outer world.

And that starts with you.

Your Journey Begins

Now that you know what your mission is, should you choose to accept it, let's close this book and get on with meditating our way to human happiness and planetary sustainability.

The 6 Phase Meditation is just the beginning of your beautiful personal growth journey. Once you go deeper into the 6 Phase Meditation, you will be compelled to start enhancing, optimizing, and improving every aspect of yourself. So I encourage you to practice on a daily basis.

Many people do the 6 Phase for hundreds of days in a row, and I take my hat off to them. That's optimal. But look, if you miss a day, it's not a big deal. The last thing I want to do is put another mindless checkbox on your to-do list.

Do this for you. Do it because it makes you feel good. Do it because it's going to support you as you shine your light into the world.

This meditation is by far the most effective thing I do every single day of my life, and I truly hope it becomes as much of a lifeline for you as it has for me.

So, this is my gift to you. As I've said throughout the book, the 6 Phase Meditation is completely free of charge on all the platforms we use, and it always will be. Furthermore, I want you to feel completely free to take it, hack it, change it, tweak it, teach it to your friends, squeeze it into five minutes, prolong it for thirty, do whatever you want. But there's one rule.

Make sure you get in touch with me to tell me what you did.

The 6 Phase Meditation is always evolving (it's already changed a lot in the past eight years) and I'm always looking to refine it so I can get it out there to as many people as possible. If this approach enhances your life, please help me get the word out by sharing your story on http://stories.mindvalley.com.

Closing Word: Never Give Up

Before we close out, I want to leave you with one piece of advice.

Keep going.

Even when it seems like you're plateauing a year later, even when it seems like you don't "need" the 6 Phase Meditation anymore, keep meditating.

Just like physical exercise, it will always be good for you. You don't stop walking, dancing, and lifting weights when you've got the body you always wanted, right? You keep training to maintain that hot body. It's the same with your mind.

John Davy, the brilliant entrepreneur behind Jongleurs, a world-famous chain of comedy clubs based in the United Kingdom, once told me that he practiced the 6 Phase Meditation for a hundred days in a row.

After one hundred days, it goes without saying that meditating started to feel quite normal. He wasn't noticing the huge shifts he was before, so he decided to stop. He was a busy man, after all.

Only thereafter, his colleagues and friends began gradually approaching him with concern.

"John, are you okay?"

"John, there's something up."

"John, are you off your medication?"

He wasn't even on any to begin with. He had no idea what they were talking about. But his friends shared that they'd noticed that he'd become more fidgety and was visibly returning to old, anxious patterns.

He realized that it had been his meditation practice counteracting those unhealthy habits and regulating his energy and success as a leader. Needless to say, he returned to his practice.

So keep going when the going is easy. But you also want to keep going when things go wrong. *Especially* when things go wrong.

I really wish I could wave a magic wand and assure you that, because you bought this book, you'll become the twenty-first-century incarnation of the Buddha or a younger version of Gandhi. That's to say that you'll instantly become so enlightened that nothing will ever bother you again. That you'll never get your heart broken again; that you'll never suffer loss, stress, and turbulence. That you'll never experience resistance to meditation. That you'll never dread sitting in a quiet room with your own head when you're at your worst.

I can't wave that magic wand, and neither would it be just.

Because sometimes—a lot of the time, actually—it's through pain that we extract our deepest wisdom and inner knowing. We will always *grow* through what we *go* through if we're open to becoming bigger than what happens "to" us and to upleveling our consciousness.

No, I don't know what's in store for you when you close this book, nor do I know what's in store for me when I finish writing it.

But I do know one thing.

I know that no matter what, we now have a set of skills that won't just allow us to survive our biggest setbacks—we have a set of skills that will enable us to *thrive*, achieve, and prosper as a species.

THE 6 PHASE MEDITATION TRANSCRIPT

This final section includes my script for the 6 Phase Meditation to allow you to practice this meditation in educational contexts and to provide extra accessibility for readers who may be deaf or hard of hearing.

Welcome to the 6 Phase Meditation.

I'm Vishen Lakhiani, and I'm going to gently guide you through all six phases of this exercise.

We will begin with Phase 1: The Circle of Love and Compassion. I want you to bring to mind someone whom you truly love. This may be a family member, a friend, a lover, or even a pet.

See this soul in front of you. And as you do so, feel the love that they fill you with. Feel that love in your heart.

Now, give this love a color. Perhaps a light green, pink, white, or blue.

Now take a deep breath. And as you exhale, imagine this light of love expanding from your heart area to fill your entire body.

Take another deep breath. And as you do, feel the light of this love move out from beyond your body to fill the room that you're currently in.

And as this light expands to fill the room, imagine this feeling of love emanating from you to all life in the room; to every person, every pet, even every plant.

Now take a deep breath. And as you exhale, imagine this light of love filling the entire building, touching everything that represents life within the building.

Take a deep breath. And as you exhale, imagine this love emanating further to cover the entire city you're in. You may feel a sense of the city or see the city as if you were looking at it on a map. See the city covered in the light of this love and compassion.

Again take a deep breath. And as you exhale, feel this light of love fill the entire country that you're in. As you did for your city, you may see the country as if you're looking at it on a map, or you could even bring to mind your nation's flag.

Imagine your love and compassion emanating from your heart to every human being, animal, and plant within this country.

Take another deep breath. And as you exhale, allow your love and compassion to expand so much that it covers the entire planet.

See the entire globe in front of you with all its countries, people, animals, and plants covered with the light of your love.

You may even repeat a blessing or a mantra for every living creature on Earth, such as:

May you be well, may you be free of suffering, may you be at peace.

You've now completed Phase 1.

We now move to Phase 2: Happiness and Gratitude.

I want you to bring to mind three things that you're grateful for in your personal life.

They could have happened in the past day, week, month, year, or even years ago. As you reflect on those three things, focus on the emotions they bring out in you. Feel the joy, the love, the lightness, and the appreciation that you felt the moment you received these gifts or lived these experiences.

Now think about your work life. Think about three things that you can be grateful for in your career that perhaps happened within the last twenty-four hours or seven days.

Whether you're appreciating a kind word from a coworker, a project going well, or the income you made, feel all the positive emotions and give thanks.

And now we move to the third level of gratitude: gratitude for yourself.

Think about three aspects of your being. These could be related to your body, your mind, aspects of your personality, anything you're grateful for about yourself.

Give thanks and gratitude for these three aspects of yourself, feeling the joy and the positive emotions as you bring to mind each unique aspect of you.

We now come to Phase 3: Peace Through Forgiveness.

Think of some incident or some occasion that caused a negative charge to build within you. It could be something small or something big. But if you're just starting out, start with something minor. See that person whom you need to forgive standing in front of you in a safe space in your mind.

It could be a beach, a forest, or a garden, wherever you feel safe.

Look at them and express how you feel. Tell them exactly what they did to harm or betray you as if you were reading the charge out in court.

For a few moments, allow yourself to feel the pain.

Now stop focusing on the pain and again draw your attention to the person who wronged you. Try to see it from their eyes, as difficult as this may initially seem. Think about how they may have perceived the situation. You can go further and think about what they could have experienced in their life that caused them to behave in this way. Remember, hurt people hurt people.

After you've seen the situation from their eyes, reflect on what you may have learned from this incident.

How did it help you grow? Did this incident help you become stronger or wiser?

And now, as you see this person in front of you, choose to forgive them.

If you can, imagine giving them a hug as a symbol of your forgiveness.

You may repeat this process with the same incident and the same person every day as you do the 6 Phase, depending on the gravity of the incident. When you feel like you can hug the person with no negative charge, you can move on to another person.

We now come to Phase 4: A Vision for Your Future. I want you to bring to mind your visions and your dreams for your life three years ahead.

Remember, we often overestimate what we can do in one year, but underestimate what we can do in three. So visualize your life three years from now as if it were a movie playing out on a screen in front of you. Bring to mind any area of your life that you care about.

You may run through a perfect scene of your life three years from now, or you may choose two or three specific goals that you have for yourself. These could be connected to your career, your love life, your health, your fitness, where you wish to travel . . . they could be goals linked to your personal growth or spirituality.

Either way, make the visions of these goals as vivid as you can. Bring in all five senses. What do you see? If your vision isn't your dominant sense, what can you hear? What can you smell? What sensations and feelings can you feel?

Think about this goal as if it's already happening.

I will give you a few minutes to linger with your future visions. Remember to bring in all five senses.

What do you see?

What do you hear?

What do you feel, smell, and taste?

Who else is in the scene with you?

It helps to see other people benefit from your accomplishments.

As you wrap up, know that this future vision is on its way to you.

We now go to Phase 5: Mastering Your Day.

Think of your day as a series of stages or segments. You're about to see each section unfold with perfect intention.

We'll start with your morning just after you've completed your meditation. If you're meditating at night, this will be the morning you're waking up to.

Set an intention for how you would want your morning to unfold.

What's the first thing you're doing? Perhaps you see your morning exercises going wonderfully. Maybe you taste your delicious, nourishing breakfast on your tongue . . . see your working, studying, or leisure day going perfectly. See the time progressing—9 a.m., 10 a.m., 11 a.m. . . .

See smiling faces around you; see beautiful synchronicities coming to pass and feelings of ease and joy.

See your lunchtime going beautifully, feeling inspired, deeply connected with yourself and those around you, peaceful and positive.

You may bring to mind specific meetings or events you have happening during the day and set an intention for each of these to flow as you'd like them to.

See the time progressing—2 p.m., 3 p.m., 4 p.m., 5 p.m. . . .

As you wrap up your day, perhaps see yourself returning home or meeting with loved ones, enjoying laughter, relaxation, joy, and happiness.

See your evening time going wonderfully.

And now see yourself going to bed, about to have a wonderful, refreshing, healthy night's sleep.

You've now completed Phase 5.

We now go to Phase 6: The Blessing.

You'll now ask for a blessing to conclude your practice and to support you on your life's journey today.

Take a moment to connect to whatever higher power you believe in, whether that's a certain deity, the universe, the "field"—whichever word you use to describe your higher power. If you're an atheist, see an older, wiser version of yourself blessing you and your intentions.

Imagine this blessing as a beautiful golden or white light shining down from above. Allow this light to travel its way through your head all the way down your spine, all the way down to the tips of your toes.

Now, imagine this light expanding from your body to form a bubble around you, enveloping you in a shield of loving, infinitely powerful light sent by your higher power. Know that this blessing will be with you for the rest of your day to protect you from negativity, support you, and fill you with all the qualities you need to flourish.

This is your blessing.

You have now completed the 6 Phase Meditation.

I'm now going to count from one to five. When I reach the count of five, you'll be wide awake, feeling wonderful, in perfect health, feeling better than before.

One, two, three . . . get ready to open your eyes at the count of five feeling wonderful, in perfect health, feeling better than before, four, five . . . eyes open, wide awake, feeling alert, wonderful, positive, refreshed, better than before.

This is Vishen Lakhiani, and thank you for joining me in the 6 Phase Meditation.

NOTES

Preface

***Billboard* magazine wrote a fascinating article:** Mitchell, Gail, "Miguel Talks Connecting with Fans Through Meditation Before His Shows," *Billboard*, 26 Sept. 2018, https://www.billboard.com/music/rb-hip-hop /miguel-meditation-interview-8477080/.

xviii **"Only 15% of the world's":** Gallup Inc., "The World's Broken Workplace," Gallup.com, 13 June 2017, https://news.gallup.com/opinion /chairman/212045/world-broken-workplace.aspx.

Introduction

5 **Since 2012 the number of people:** "27 Meditation Statistics: Data and Trends Revealed for 2022," *The Good Body*, 13 Jan. 2022, https://www .thegoodbody.com/meditation-statistics/.

12 **It boosts energy:** Allen, Summer, "The Science of Gratitude," Greater Good Science Center, UC Berkeley, 2018, https://ggsc.berkeley.edu/images /uploads/GGSC-JTF_White_Paper-Gratitude-FINAL.pdf.

13 **What's more, research is now showing:** Carson, James W., et al., "Forgiveness and Chronic Low Back Pain: A Preliminary Study Examining the Relationship of Forgiveness to Pain, Anger, and Psychological Distress," *Journal of Pain*, vol. 6, no. 2, Feb. 2005, pp. 84–91, DOI.org (Crossref), https://doi.org/10.1016/j.jpain.2004.10.012.

16 **Take a look at the following graph**: Lakhiani, Vishen, *The Code of the Extraordinary Mind: Ten Unconventional Laws to Redefine Your Life and Succeed on Your Own Terms*, Rodale, 2016.

19 **In psychologist Shawn Achor's book**: Achor, Shawn, *The Happiness Advantage: How a Positive Brain Fuels Success in Work and Life*, Currency, 2013.

Chapter 1

38 **Did you know**: Kafko, Steven, "History Lesson—How America Started Brushing Teeth," 209 NYC Dental, 22 November 2016, https://www.209nycdental.com/history-lesson-america-started-brush-teeth/.

41 **You see, our brains are sneaky**: Tetlock, Phillip, "A Social Check on the Fundamental Attribution Error," *Social Psychology Quarterly*, vol. 48, no. 3, Sept. 1985, pp. 227–36, http://faculty.haas.berkeley.edu/tetlock/vita/Philip%20Tetlock/Phil%20Tetlock/1984-1987/1985%20Accountability%20A%20Social%20Check%20on%20the%20Fundamental%20Attri.pdf.

44 **Naming it "the Very Happy"**: Diener, Ed, and Martin E. P. Seligman, "Very Happy People," *Psychological Science*, vol. 13, no. 1, Jan. 2002, pp. 81–84, DOI.org (Crossref), https://doi.org/10.1111/1467-9280.00415.

49 **Because these awesome humans**: Davidson, Richard, "Regulation of the Neural Circuitry of Emotion by Compassion Meditation: Effects of Meditative Expertise," University of Wisconsin–Madison, 2008, https://news.wisc.edu/study-shows-compassion-meditation-changes-the-brain/#sthash.416H9FF5.dpuf.

51 **Reduced physical pain**: Weng, Helen Y., et al. "Compassion Training Alters Altruism and Neural Responses to Suffering," *Psychological Science*, vol. 24, no. 7, July 2013, pp. 1171–80. https://doi.org/10.1177/0956797612469537.

51 **Reversal of aging**: Hamilton, David R., "Loving Kindness Slows Ageing at the Genetic Level," 14 Aug. 2019, https://drdavidhamilton.com/loving-kindness-slows-ageing-at-the-genetic-level/.

52 **Studies show that**: Gregoire, C., "Kindness Really Does Make You More Attractive," *HuffPost*, 29 Oct. 2014, https://www.huffpost.com/entry/kindness-attractive_n_6063074.

52 **Your heart resonance is**: McCraty, Rollin, et al., "The Resonant Heart," HeartMath Institute, 2005, https://www.heartmath.org/research/research-library/relevant/the-resonant-heart/. Accessed 14 Feb. 2022.

Chapter 2

62   **After traveling to Japan**: Stillman, Jessica, "In 1922 Einstein Scribbled the Secret to Happiness on a Note. Nearly a Hundred Years Later It Sold for $1.56 Million," *Inc.com*, 29 Nov. 2021, https://www.inc.com /jessica-stillman/albert-einstein-happiness-theory.html.

64   **The world-renowned entrepreneurial coach**: Sullivan, Dan, and Benjamin Hardy, *The Gap and the Gain: The High Achievers' Guide to Happiness, Confidence, and Success*, Hay House, 2021.

69   **My favorite study**: Emmons, Robert A., *Thanks! How the New Science of Gratitude Can Make You Happier*, Houghton Mifflin, 2007.

71   **Enhanced feelings of life**: "Giving Thanks Can Make You Happier," Harvard Health Publishing, 22 Nov. 2011, https://www.health.harvard .edu/healthbeat/giving-thanks-can-make-you-happier.

72   **unlike at least one billion people**: OHCHR, *Annual Thematic Reports: Special Rapporteur on the Right to Adequate Housing*, United Nations, https://www.ohchr.org/EN/Issues/Housing/Pages/AnnualReports.aspx. Accessed 14 Feb. 2022.

79   **Gratitude has been strongly linked**: Wattles, W. D., *The Science of Getting Rich: Your Master Key to Success*, Thrifty Books, 2009.

Chapter 3

89   **A co-study by various universities**: Zheng, Xue, et al., "The Unburdening Effects of Forgiveness: Effects on Slant Perception and Jumping Height," *Social Psychological and Personality Science*, vol. 6, no. 4, May 2015, pp. 431–38, DOI.org (Crossref), https://doi.org/10.1177/1948550614564222.

89   **Forgiveness has also been proven**: Friedberg, Jennifer P., et al., "The Impact of Forgiveness on Cardiovascular Reactivity and Recovery," *International Journal of Psychophysiology*, vol. 65, no. 2, Aug. 2007, pp. 87–94, https://doi.org/10.1016/j.ijpsycho.2007.03.006.

91   **Long before my arrival**: "Alpha One Brain Training and Neurofeedback," Biocybernaut Institute, https://www.biocybernaut.com/training/. Accessed 14 Feb. 2022.

103   **In that book**: Walsch, Neale Donald, *The Little Soul and the Sun: A Children's Parable*, adapted from *Conversations with God*, Hampton Roads Publishing, 1998.

Chapter 4

125   **In a study conducted on basketball players**: Kearns, Dwight W., and Jane Crossman, "Effects of a Cognitive Intervention Package on the Free-Throw Performance of Varsity Basketball Players During Practice and

Competition," *Perceptual and Motor Skills*, vol. 75, no. 3 suppl., Dec. 1992, pp. 1243–53, https://doi.org/10.2466/pms.1992.75.3f.1243.

125   **A study known as**: Ranganathan, Vinoth K., et al., "From Mental Power to Muscle Power—Gaining Strength by Using the Mind," *Neuropsychologia*, vol. 42, no. 7, 2004, pp. 944–56, https://doi.org/10.1016/j.neuropsychologia .2003.11.018.

125   **tested this theory and proved**: Silva, José, and Philip Miele, *The Silva Mind Control Method*, Pocket Books, 1991.

126   **But after using creative visualization**: Simonton, O. Carl, et al., *Getting Well Again: A Step-by-Step, Self-Help Guide to Overcoming Cancer for Patients and Their Families*, J. P. Tarcher, distributed by St. Martin's Press, 1978.

127   **Strengthen your brain's neuroplasticity**: Blue Banyan AU, "Creative Visualization: The Neurology of How It Works—And How to Make It Work for You!" *Medium*, 22 April 2014, https://medium.com/@Blue BanyanAU/creative-visualization-the-neurology-of-how-it-works-and -how-to-make-it-work-for-you-8994211a7675.

Chapter 5

145   **In a nutshell, your RAS**: Bokhari, Dean, "The Power of Focusing on What You Want (How Your Brain's Reticular Activating System Functions in Your Favor)," https://www.meaningfulhq.com/reticular-activating-system -function.html. Accessed 14 Feb. 2022.

Chapter 6

154   **84 percent of humanity nonetheless believes**: "The Global Religious Landscape," Pew Research Center, Religion & Public Life Project, 18 Dec. 2012, https://www.pewforum.org/2012/12/18/global-religious-landscape -exec/.

154   **although there's no solid proof**: "Results of World's Largest Near Death Experiences Study Published," University of Southampton, 7 Oct. 2014, https://www.southampton.ac.uk/news/2014/10/07-worlds-largest -near-death-experiences-study.page. Accessed 14 Feb. 2022.

160   **Richard Dawkins, author of**: Harrison, Paul, "Adding Emotion to Atheism," *New Statesman*, 9 June 2021, https://www.newstatesman.com /politics/2008/06/universe-atheism-pantheist-god.

Chapter 7

169   **In his famous article**: Urban, Tim, "The Great Battle of Fire and Light," Wait But Why, 26 Aug. 2019, https://waitbutwhy.com/2019/08/fire-light .html.

ACKNOWLEDGMENTS

First of all, thank you so much to all my family, Hayden, Eve, Kristina, Mohan, Roopi, Virgo, and Ljubov, and to all my amazing friends who help make me who I am.

I would also like to thank all our Mindvalley authors and trainers who have nurtured me with wisdom and facilitated my personal growth for more than two decades now, and who inspired many teachings in this book.

Big thanks to the team at Penguin Random House and Donna Loffredo for your unwavering professionalism and support; I'm truly honored to have worked so closely with you on this project.

And last but not least, to my coeditor and collaborator Amy White: the foul-mouthed Brit with a brilliant sense of humor who helped me put this book together. Thank you for compiling my ideas, translating them into the written word, as well as cracking the whip that kept me on time.

INDEX

ABOUT THE AUTHOR

VISHEN LAKHIANI is the founder and CEO of Mind-valley, the world's most powerful transformation platform with a growing community of twenty million and a mission to help people step into their greatness. He is the author of the *New York Times* bestsellers *The Buddha and the Badass* and *The Code of the Extraordinary Mind,* which has been translated into more than twenty languages.

Scan this QR code to unlock your FREE
Online 6 Phase Meditation Program.

More from *New York Times* bestselling author

VISHEN LAKHIANI

THE BUDDHA AND THE BADASS

THE SECRET SPIRITUAL ART OF SUCCEEDING AT WORK

NEW YORK TIMES BESTSELLER

VISHEN LAKHIANI
Bestselling Author of *The Code of the Extraordinary Mind*

10 UNCONVENTIONAL LAWS TO REDEFINE YOUR LIFE & SUCCEED ON YOUR OWN TERMS

NEW YORK TIMES BESTSELLER

THE **CODE** OF THE **EXTRAORDINARY MIND**

"This book will make you question everything you thought you knew about your life."
—DAVE ASPREY, FOUNDER OF BULLETPROOF 360

VISHEN LAKHIANI
FOUNDER OF MINDVALLEY

RODALE
BOOKS

Available wherever books are sold